C0-AUK-630

A Picture Dictionary for the Home Gardener

A Picture Dictionary for the HOME GARDENER

by

Andrée Vilas Grabe

BRAMHALL HOUSE : NEW YORK

Library of Congress catalog card number: 63–11053

This edition published by Bramhall House,
a division of Clarkson N. Potter, Inc.,
by arrangement with Hill & Wang
(A)

Manufactured in the United States of America

About this Book

The world of gardening has undergone radical changes in the past ten years. The mass exodus from city to country has bred a whole new generation of gardeners who, more often than not, have never had a trowel in their hands. To help these poor souls, a plethora of "timesaving" equipment has appeared on the market, confusing the mind and cluttering up the garage; and a veritable rash of gardening books has broken out. These range all the way from the definitive, telling you in detail just which timesavers to use to do any number of backbreaking jobs, to those advising you to throw the whole darned mess away and just mulch!

Even more perplexing is one's almost daily exposure to the tantalizing array of plants that now abound on the shelves of supermarkets, dime stores, hardware stores, discount stores, and roadside stands. There, you're really on your own—and at sea. What is it? Is it hardy? How big will it get? Does it need sun? Will it come up again next year? Don't bother to ask the man. He just sells them.

This book is an effort to help you find the answers. The second section is a simple reference to the individual care and culture of some 850 plants. Plants are grouped into familiar categories such as perennials, ground covers, vines, hedges, etc., to make it easy for you to find a given type of plant to do a specific job. And, in case you don't know to which category a plant belongs, there is also an alphabetical listing of all plants starting on page 152 which will tell you where to find the information you want.

The first section is largely a how-to section covering well-known garden subjects such as planning, planting, propagation, etc. But with one difference. For my aim here was not only to give you ways and means to grow plants easily and with a minimum of work but to suggest something far more intangible—how to have a garden.

Intangible and ambitious, I fear, for a garden is such a personal thing. It is part of a whole complex of amorphous feelings we have for the need to live with the sky above and the earth below. In this sense, a garden is not just a display of flowers, an evergreen hedge, a shady tree. Nor is it how to build a rock wall, or a barbecue, or a pool for goldfish and waterlilies. A garden is an emotional environment, a place that gives expression and dimension to our lives. I hope, in some way, that the opening section of this book will help you find this.

Acknowledgments

I would like to thank the following people and firms for their great help in lending me many of the photographs in this book. Photographs are identified by numbers within each section of the book.

Breck's of Boston, 250 Breck Building, Boston, Mass.: seeds, bulbs, garden equipment; catalog on request. Annuals: 1, 31.

California Redwood Association, 576 Sacramento St., San Francisco, Calif.: garden design ideas. New Ways to Garden: 9, 10, 12.

Flower Grower Magazine, 1 Park Ave., New York 16, N. Y.: jacket color photos.

C. A. Cruickshank, 1015 Mt. Pleasant Rd., Toronto, Ontario, Canada: cold-climate plants; catalog on request. Perennials 32, 71.

George W. Park Seed Co., Greenwood, S. C.: seeds, bulbs, plants; catalog on request. New Ways to Garden: 29–32; Perennials: 3, 5, 13, 16, 19, 22, 27, 53–55, 62, 63, 65, 70; Annuals: 6; Rock Garden Plants: 1, 6, 13, 21; Trailers: 3, 9; Vines and Climbers: 6, 8; Shrubs: 42.

Jackson and Perkins Co., Newark, N. Y.: specialists in roses; catalog on request. Vines: 12; Shrubs: 30, 43–45.

Merry Gardens, 1 Simonton Rd., Camden, Me.: rare geraniums, begonias, tropicals; catalog on request. Perennials and Biennials: 29; Shrubs, Trees, Hedges: 18, 21.

Musser Forests, Inc., Indiana, Pa.: excellent trees, shrubs, hedges; catalog on request. New Ways to Garden: 33; Shrubs: 3, 5, 7, 8, 12, 13, 15, 20, 23–26, 29, 33–35, 38, 40, 41, 47, 49, 50, 51, 53, 54.

Netherlands Flower-Bulb Institute: hardy Holland bulbs; consult local dealers. Perennials and Biennials: 1, 17, 18, 37, 77–79; Rock Garden Plants: 28, 30, 31, 33; Trailers, Ground Covers, Creepers: 5.

Organic Gardening and Farming Magazine, Emmaus, Pa. New Ways to Garden: 28, 38; Annuals: 38.

Pearce Seed Co., Moorestown, N. J.: interesting bulbs and perennials; catalog on request. Perennials: 75, 80.

Stern's Nurseries, Geneva, N. Y.: plants, shrubs, trees; catalog on request. Shrubs 17, 46.

W. Atlee Burpee Co., Philadelphia 2, Pa.: seed growers; catalog on request. New Ways to Garden: 20–27; Perennials: 4, 7–12, 14, 21, 23, 24, 28, 31, 34, 36, 48, 50, 52, 57, 61, 66–69, 72–74; Annuals: 2–5, 7–27, 29–34, 36, 37, 39–42; Rock Garden Plants: 2–5, 7, 10, 20, 23, 26, 27; Trailers: 10; Vines: 2, 4, 5, 10, 13; Shrubs: 27.

Walter Marx Gardens, Boring, Oreg.: irises and lilies; catalog on request. Perennials: 2, 6, 20, 30, 35, 38–45, 47, 49, 51, 56, 59, 60, 64; Annuals: 28; Rock Garden Plants: 9, 34.

In addition, I would like to thank the following people for their help as follows:

Carolyn Brown for her helping me cover the coastal areas of the South. Mrs. Brown is the proprietor of Pelican Cove, Islamorada, Florida Keys, Fla., the winter refuge of professors, publishers, bird watchers, and itinerant writer's like myself.

James C. Rose, landscape architect, for the loan of his excellent photographs on garden design. Author of *Creative Gardens*, Mr. Rose may be reached through his publishers: Reinhold Publishing Co., 430 Park Ave., New York 22, N. Y.

Walter Miles, graphic artist and author of *Designs for Craftsmen*, for permitting me to photograph his lovely gardens.

Stanley F. Bulpitt of Brookside Nurseries, Darien, Conn., for allowing me to photograph his extensive collection of hardy ground covers, and rock garden plants.

Contents

New Ways to Garden

Any homeowner who has moved to the country within the last decade cannot help but be painfully aware of how many others have sought refuge in the wide-open places. Homes and housing developments have mushroomed everywhere within reasonable commuting distance (now stretched to two hours, often with a twenty-minute drive to the station), with the result that most of us feel downright lucky if we're left with a little more than a front and a back yard. The country is rapidly becoming the suburbs and the suburbs the city.

While our desires for more space, more fresh air, more relaxation, more privacy, more rest mount, properties become smaller and smaller with fewer trees, less privacy, less peace and quiet. And expensive! No longer can we gaze out the window at the unbroken countryside or seek a quiet nook in the woods or a pretty spot for a picnic or send the kids out to play in the fields. We have to make our own vistas, our own quiet corners, our own outdoor living and dining rooms, and some place where the children can play without trampling all over the flower beds of an irate neighbor.

Compounding the problem is the inexorable factor—time! With fathers putting in a twelve-hour day (7 A.M. to 7 P.M. is par from home to office and back) and mothers putting in anywhere between a thirteen- to sixteen-hour day (dinner dishes must be washed, the kids put to bed—and there's always a Meeting), there's little, if ever, more free time than week ends. Some work in the garden is refreshing, if only as a respite from the frantic work week. But solid week ends of mowing, hoeing, weeding, watering, week after week, are something else again. Besides, Dad promised to take Johnny to the baseball game, or fishing or bowling or the movies. And Mother's got a list of things for Dad to do around the house—a *long* list.

Like many homeowners you've probably already given up the vegetable garden (and, whether your wife knows it or not, next year the flower garden is scheduled for a drastic cutback). But how about the lawn? How about the seeding and the topsoil and the rolling and the crabgrass and the mowing and the trimming and the watering?

Before you throw the baby out with the bath water please look at the pictures on the following pages.

1. *From* Creative Gardening, *James C. Rose, Reinhold Publ. Corp.*

This could be just another side and back of a house on a small property. Instead it is a lovely, spacious, private garden. In place of the usual small back yards with grass and flowers and useless sides with foundation planting hugging the house, every inch of ground has been carpeted in stone in one continuous panoramic sweep. A difficult sloping bank around the property has been turned into three attractive levels, with trees, shrubs, flowers, and stones strategically placed to screen the home from the eyes of neighbors and passers-by, to add color and form to the garden, and to give ample space for dining, lounging, or play. Maintenance? Outside occasional watering in dry spells and sweeping up the leaves in fall, it's practically nil. A stray weed might crop up between the stone mulch on trees and shrubs and the peat mulch on flower beds but this will be rare and its roots offer little resistance. The beauty of this garden won't fade away leaving a sad tangled growth with the passing of the last flower. Stones are refreshed and washed with each shower, dark evergreens contrast handsomely with white birch all year. Expensive? Only the wood beams holding the first level—the second layer is flat wood-board—will cost any real money, but so would a rock wall or other device—and at least here you've got something for your money! Gravel (smashed stones, smooth, rounded stones, quartz or marble chips in many handsome colors as well as white and black) costs little or no more than topsoil and you'll only need about half as much. And there's no cost for grass seed, fertilizer, etc., initially or year after year. No need for a lawnmower or other expensive garden tools. A hand trowel, spade, rake, shovel, hose, ordinary bamboo rake, a little fresh thinking, and a garden like this can be yours.

2. *Courtesy James C. Rose*

Here is real country living in miniature, complete with vegetable, fruit and flower garden, and outdoor dining room. In the foreground is a salad garden. You can make a small space like this yield generously and continuously by using extrarich topsoil—no big job in such a small space—sowing the seed close together and eating the thinnings as you go along. As soon as a hole appears throw in a handful of fresh topsoil and sprinkle some seed for a succession of crops. The board fence separating the lounging and dining area from the vegetable area supports tomato plants and cucumber vines on one side, is bordered by flowering shrubs and flowers on the other side. The ground is inlaid with concrete block (no maintenance) placed irregularly to make an interesting design as well as to contain plants. Here is privacy, room for play and relaxation, infinite charm. Gardening in a spot like this is pure pleasure. It's easy to overlook the potential of a tiny space like this. It could be your entire space, of course. Often it's a dismissed "unusable" corner of helter-skelter trees, shrubs, and flowers. Outside your kitchen door? Side door? Den? Downstairs bedroom?

3. *Courtesy James C. Rose*

If you've lost your view, make one. It doesn't take an estate or rolling hills, or vast horticultural displays or a swimming pool to bring peace and enchantment into your life. Here you can feast your eyes on a pretty pattern of trees and shrubs and flowers, gaze at the lazy goldfish in a sunlit pond. When the little fountain is turned on, swarms of birds appear adding their song to the tinkle of the waterfall—and, incidentally, gobbling up pesky insects! Pretty small—pretty wonderful. In spring you can clean out the pool before you fill it —and there goes your work for the year!

Sticks and stones won't break your bones. They are handsome, versatile and undemanding. Here are some of the ways you can use them to make life easier and more attractive:

4.

Two sizes of stones separated by crosscut logs give an interesting contrast of colors and textures, divide a garden walk from a planted area. No weeds, no trimming of edges, no mud to track into the house.

5.

A grass area near the house is kept small and easy to maintain (but note that even it needs cutting!) by the imaginative use of stone, logs, natural rocks and boulders.

6.

Unmanageable, unearthed boulders become modern sculpture. Those in the background serve to hold back a small mulched planted area. White stones, black peat, green shrubs, bold boulders—a nondescript spot becomes a thing of beauty and a joy to maintain.

7.

An undesirable and "difficult" bump becomes the stage for a peninsula of plants and deep black mulch in a sea of white quartz chips.

8. *Courtesy James C. Rose*

Stones used in place of ground cover to hold back a bank stay trim and tidy without work, form a handsome setting for trees.

Stones used as a mulch for shrubs and trees control weeds, prevent parching and baking of soil, keep plants evenly cool and moist in summer, and protect them from alternate harmful freezing and thawing (heaving) in winter. You'll save money by first spreading the cheapest grade of gravel and then topping it with a fine grade. White quartz or white marble chips are truly beautiful with green foliage.

9.

10.

Small plot to rich man's garden. Even a tiny house on a tiny piece of land can have gardens, pools, space for dining, for sunning in charming seclusion. Here is a wealth of flowering shrubs, evergreens, and flowers held to a judicious low-maintenance level—a kind of sunken garden surrounded by decks for lounging and dining. Birds, attracted by the little waterfall, complete the picture. If you have more space, wouldn't this make a nice tea house and garden in some corner of your land?

11. *Courtesy James C. Rose*

If you can't tame it, pave it. Poor soil, no sun, lots of rocks and boulders—a classic setting for nothing but straggly weeds becomes an enchanting rustic garden. Bricks are worked in and around the boulders, green ground cover into nooks and crannies, young trees into sunlit spots. Lunch anyone?

12.

An impossibly steep bank with an old gnarled tree becomes a double-decker garden with lovely plants, privacy, room for outdoor living on two levels. Here, redwood is used as a platform for a second level, but take away the steep bank and you have an example of what you can do in any two-by-four back yard. Stones, cement blocks, flagstones, thin crosscuts of large, round logs, any number of things could be used for the floor. No upkeep—just enjoy it!

13. *Courtesy James C. Rose*

You can have your lawn and enjoy it too if you restrict it to a manageable area. Here lawn and concrete blocks are combined to curtail relentless lawn maintenance, while providing that cool pleasant feeling of green-carpeted space.

14.

A house smack on the road with no land at all gains privacy and outdoor living space—even a vegetable and flower garden. Forty dollars in lumber made the sundeck which is high enough to protect the people sitting in low beach chairs from the view of passers-by, low enough to keep within "regulations." Small flat boards form a planter to hold the climbing tomato plants, lettuce parsley, chives, and gaily colored rose moss. The sundeck is ringed on the inside with a complete flower and vegetable garden in pots; potted hardy evergreens are substituted in the winter. Outdoors in the summer are gardenias, camellias, bougainvillea, flowering maples, masses of pink and white geraniums (the quickest way to instant gardens that I know), plus a sprinkling of potted "annuals"—fragrant nicoteanas, hybrid petunias; tomatoes, peppers, lettuce, chervil, shallots, parsley, and water cress in various pots and flower boxes (see page 12). The door is framed with heavenly blue morning glories rising from a container of massed caladium.

15.

Water cress in a flower box grows in abundance in equal parts of loam, sand, and peat, with a little sheep or cow manure (the packaged kind) thrown in. Keep moist and in the shade. Plants are readily available. Next time you buy water cress at your grocery store simply root a few sprigs in water.

16.

Leaf lettuce will grow and grow and grow in a rich house-plant mixture of equal parts of sand, peat, and soil mixed with a little fertilizer. As you eat the lettuce, drop a handful of soil with a few seeds into the bare spot for a succession of crops.

17.

Tomatoes planted in large pots yield a generous harvest of delicious fruit if grown in full sun and rich soil. Fertilize regularly and don't let them dry out. It's a good way to get an interesting and tasty variety, too! Shown here are cherry tomatoes.

18. *Courtesy James C. Rose*

Ground cover without upkeep. Two sizes of stones merging into each other relieve monotony, create pace and interest, keep the ground looking neat without work. A very good solution for spots where nothing else will grow, such as those beneath large thirsty trees that rob all nearby plants of water.

19.

Instant gardens with potted plants. This is a well-known device in tropical climates—an idea well worth borrowing by Northern neighbors who have to summer indoor plants outdoors. And don't restrict yourself to flowers. Many vegetables and fruits grow well in pots too—all they need is a good rich soil mixture, adequate sun, and faithful attention to watering. How about a potted herb garden of fennel, sweet marjoram, dill, sweet basil, lavender, parsley?

20. SWEET MARJORAM

21. DILL

22. SWEET BASIL

23. LAVENDER

24. RADISHES

25. CUCUMBERS

You don't have to have a vegetable garden to grow vegetables. They are plants, too, and can be grown right along with other plants. Just be sure they get full sun. The bright green tops of young radishes make an attractive low border. Cucumbers and tomatoes can make a ground cover; or they can be trained to grow up as vines.

Chives are easily grown in pots or in the open ground. One clump will yield fragrant seasonings all summer long. The more you cut the more it grows.

26.

27.

You can grow surprisingly large quantities of snap beans and limas if you get pole types and grow them as a vine. And as you can see, peas can be trained to climb, too.

The Soil; Planting; Transplanting

If you garden as suggested above there'll be no necessity to lay out and prepare large planting beds with rigid timetables—no laborious spading, turning over soil, breaking up clumps, smoothing, pulverizing, leveling, when and if the ground is ready to work. You can work one small space at a time, planting as much or as little as you have the time and inclination for.

THE SOIL: The better it is, the healthier, handsomer, more vigorous, more insect- and disease-resistant the plant, and the less time you'll spend fussing over it later. Unless you live in a notoriously acid, or alkaline, soil area, forget the mysteries of the *p*H factor. What you're after is tilth or texture, a rich, spongy, easily workable soil (see picture 28). This will automatically contain ample organic matter (plant life in various stages of decomposition), which in turn will sustain a host of microscopic organisms dedicated to transforming the minerals in your soil into nutrients for your plants. Compost, of course, is ideal, but somehow one never gets around to making a compost pile: a layer cake of decaying vegetation, manure, soil, and lime, kept moist and well-aerated, which you turn over from time to time, until thoroughly decomposed.

The next best thing is to take the soil you have and add to it what it needs. How can you tell? Texture is the clue. Feel it. Squeeze it. A clay soil will be thick, gooey, clumpy, heavy when wet, hard as a rock when dry. A sandy soil won't hold its shape when wet and dribbles through your fingers when dry.

Although both may contain minerals (indeed, the clay soil may have a wealth of minerals!), plants will suffer from malnutrition. The clay soil permits little or no air to pass, and without air the bacteria that make minerals available to plant roots cannot live. It is slow to absorb water and then holds it to the point of stagnation. The sandy soil is like a sieve. It can't hold on to anything—water or nutrients.

If you could only mix them! The sandy soil would break up the clay soil and the clay soil would hold the sandy soil together. Yet, you still wouldn't have good soil because the most important single element is missing—organic matter. I can't stress this enough because organic matter is the ingredient which will make your soil the happy ground for plant growth. Its slow and steady decomposition provides long-term food for plants, fluffs (aerates) the soil, and retains water like a sponge.

Briefly then: (1) Add organic matter to sandy soil. (2) Add organic matter and sand to clay soil. (3) Add plant food to both for immediate fertility.

"Digging it in deeply," as they say, is ideal—for the soil but not for your back, particularly if your soil is heavy. I have a clay soil which I defy anyone to dig. The only time you can sink a spade in it is when it's sopping wet, which, as everybody knows, is anathema. Well, nature doesn't dig either; she just piles it on. So that's what I do. I make my own soil in one of those scoop-type wheelbarrows and simply roll it about planting and spreading the soil as I go. This way you can telescope eons of nature's handiwork. I mix equal parts of (1) my own poor soil; (2) store-packaged humus, peat, peat moss, and leaf mold (gathered from under the trees—that half-decomposed stuff right under last season's fall of leaves); (3) builder's sand. (Not the fine white sand sold for sandpiles. It must be rough. Seashore sand is all right if you wash all salt from it.) (4) Then I throw in several generous handfuls of packaged manure: cow, sheep, chicken, whatever I find in the stores, and a little "complete" commercial fertilizer—probably silly, since why add more minerals to those already in the soil? I only add lime or acid fertilizer if I know a plant really *needs* a soil that is on the alkaline or acid side. And then, but a sprinkling at a time, to *just* the amount of mixture I'm using, not to the whole mixture.

28. GOOD SOIL

Planting consists of hacking out the biggest hole I can with a hand trowel (for trees and shrubs which require spade and shovel, I draft my husband), replacing the soil I remove (into the wheelbarrow it goes for subsequent mixing) with my Ideal Planting Mix, and shaping a hole large enough to accommodate the plant.

Now (1) Water. (2) Set the plant in at the same depth it was before. Firm it in; press hard. Don't leave any air pockets. If planting stiff roots of bare-rooted trees and shrubs, you'll have to work the soil in between the roots with your hands, your feet, and if that doesn't work, flush the soil down sharply with a hose. (3) More water (to settle down the whole thing). Inevitably there's always some spill-over extra mix which I spread over the soil of adjacent plants. After several seasons of this spreading and planting of soil on the installment plan you'll be amazed at the deep, luxurious, fertile loam you have.

This, in essence, is the way you can plant anything: seedlings; plantlets; potted plants; bulbs; perennials; and deciduous trees and shrubs. Balled and burlapped evergreens (called "B and B") can go in, burlap and all—just set the root ball at the right depth in the hole, untie the burlap and let fall to bottom of hole. A mulch of peat or peat moss (there are many on the market, some a rich humusy, attractive black) will greatly inhibit the growth of weeds and make those that do appear, easy to pull out. Mulch will keep plants evenly moist and cool in the summer, protect them in the winter . . . slowly work its way into the soil to fertilize it and become a veritable mecca for thousands of little gardeners who will till the soil for you—earthworms.

Of course, you don't have to garden piecemeal like this. You may prefer to prepare the entire planting area at once. But the principle of topdressing a recalcitrant soil instead of deep-digging-and-mixing still applies.

In *most* cases! Spots that have no drainage—hardpan, it's called—a kind of hard-baked layer in the subsoil through which water can't pass, will either have to be dug up and broken up with stones and gravel if you insist on growing something there. (Sometimes whole networks of drainage pipes are put in.) Or you can simply spread stones over the spot and plant a bird bath. A very loose sandy soil should have the materials worked in to a reasonable depth. Fortunately, it's easy to dig. Naturally, you won't add sand to the mixture. And again, naturally, if your soil is good to begin with, you won't bother to do anything but use it as is.

Incidentally, even a soil that is almost pure sand can be made to grow flowers, vegetables, trees, and shrubs. Anchor the plant in a grocery bushel basket filled with soil mixture and plant the whole basket, which will slowly decompose. Topdress and mulch between baskets. Do it again next year. If you can get the kids to systematically bury the garbage (discarded vegetables, fruits, leaves, peelings, coffee grounds, eggshells—anything except tin cans and plastic, metal and heavy wrapping papers) do that, too. Ditto with the ashes in the fireplace, and the fallen leaves in autumn. If you did this long enough you could even restore the Sahara to the lush verdant land it once was. The bushel-basket method is also a good way to start trees and shrubs on a steep gravelly or sandy hill.

PLANTING SEEDS INDOORS: This is often recommended in early spring to get a head start on perennials, biennials, and annuals when one doesn't have a cold frame or hotbed. There are perils: (1) A hostile environment—too much heat, too little humidity, not enough light. (2) Human avarice. Even the most seasoned gardener can't help trying to get the most for his money. One always sows seeds too thickly, ending up with a multitude of weak, wan, leggy seedlings instead of a few squat, green, sturdy ones. (3) Nursing—forget to water, they dry up. Water too much, they rot. (4) Timing. You've got to start seeds at just the right time so they can be transplanted outdoors before they get too big (and weak)—and just when is the last frost?

I don't want to make planting sound impossible. It isn't. I do it all the time. Just be realistic. If you've got the site, the time, the desire, you'll develop the feel, the proverbial green thumb. If you don't, your local nursery can provide you with robust pedigreed plantlets. Name tags are usually in formidable Latin and are not always strictly according to Hoyle but are generally close enough so you'll know what you're getting (take this book along). Plants grown from the seeds of reputable houses cost little or no more and are worth looking for.

If you want something a little out of the ordinary you'll probably have to order it by mail. Some houses specialize in the growing of certain plants alone; others sell a large variety. (See the list on page vi.) Send for catalogs, if only for browsing pleasure.

29–30. SEED STARTING KITS

You can also buy complete kits for starting seeds like those shown in pictures 29 and 30. They come in various shapes and sizes, are not costly, and eliminate all assembling of materials and most of the guesswork.

Plants and plantlets are available in myriad other places, as I've mentioned before, but it can be trick-or-treat. Check the name tag. If there isn't any, maybe you'd better skip it, unless you know the plant and are sure that it's in good condition. Above all, I'd avoid the poor pale sprouted perennials in gaily colored cardboard and cellophane packages. Dormant (unsprouted) roots or bulbs and other tuberous perennials, however, can survive this kind of storage for a time—a *reasonable* length of time.

To start seeds you'll need:

1. A container *with drainage* (imperative!). Flowerpots are fine but they don't hold much. Seed flats are ideal but they drip. Those molded cardboardlike small pots (some are peat or dehydrated manure), now so widely available, are great because you can plant the pot as well as the plantlet and thus minimize injury to the roots in transplanting. But naturally, these pots disintegrate with watering. Several can be squeezed into a flowerpot (more in a seed flat) and held together by soil worked in the interstices. I sometimes plant molded cardboard egg containers, putting one or two seeds in each nook, and separating the nooks complete with plantlet at the time of transplanting.

2. Planting mix. Light porous materials, preferably sterile, are usually recommended. Sand, peat moss, a half and half mixture of each, vermiculite or sphagnum moss are all adequate. I use my garden mix. Since my time is not always my own, my seedlings have to be transplanted when I'm ready—and I find I can hold them off much longer in a mix that contains nutrients than in one that doesn't.

31. PELLETED SEED

3. Seed. The best you can buy! And here, I would strongly suggest you order by mail from an established house. You're sure to get viable seed and the instructions for planting are apt to be explicit. This is important because seeds vary widely in their period of germination; some are hard to grow, some easy;

some need special treatment. Pelleted seed, seed coated to increase its size, is now available (see picture 31). It helps reduce the unavoidable too thick planting of very fine seed.

Planting is easy. Before you fill a container with planting mix, put a thin layer of drainage material, such as sand or pebbles, on the bottom. If you plant in a flowerpot, first lay a broken piece of pot, hump side up, to keep the mixture from dribbling out. Level the mix. Tamp it down firmly. A wooden block, small box, or what-have-you is fine for this. I generally use the palm of my hand. If you're sowing in drills, make little planting rows no more than a quarter to a half inch deep. (The point of a pencil works well, as does your finger.) If you're broadcasting (sprinkling seed around to cover a given area), just barely loosen the soil surface with a fork or your fingertips. Now seed, sparingly, cover loosely with soil, and tamp down. I don't even cover very fine seed—just tamp them down into the mixture.

Now water. A fine even spray is usually recommended, but if you just don't happen to have a fine even sprayer around you can let water seep in from the sides. If you're planting in a flowerpot, simply set it in a saucer of water and let the soil absorb it. When the top surface is wet, drain off the excess water from the saucer.

Seeds will germinate more quickly if they are kept covered (don't exclude air), but this is tricky and they'll also germinate without covering. Always keep the soil damp but never sopping wet or the seedlings will rot. The euphemism for this is "damping off." Thin the seedlings, the sooner the better, I've found, so they'll have plenty of growing room. Eyebrow tweezers are helpful for this.

32. SEPARATING SEEDLINGS

TRANSPLANTING SEEDS OUTDOORS: Before you do, "harden" the plantlets by setting them outside in their containers for a couple of days in the sun or semi-sun depending upon the requirements of the plant, which are given in the dictionary section of this book. *Watch out that the plantlets don't dry out.* Choose a cloudy day or the early evening for the transplanting operation. If you've grown the plants in individual pots, plant pot and all as mentioned above. If not, you'll have to separate the plants. Just ease them apart gently. (Seedlings grown in a loose medium are easily separated, as shown in picture 32.) Even so, you'll tear some roots, but if you watch the plants carefully for a few days and keep the ground evenly moist at all times, they'll re-establish themselves in short order. Shading the plantlets is helpful but not always so easy to do. I find a man's umbrella anchored to the ground with a sturdy rock one of the simplest ways of shading—except in a high wind! You can move it around with the sun as need be.

Planting, itself, always sounds more complicated than it is. I've already explained my wheelbarrow method. The important thing is that the soil be good and of a fine consistency. Make a hole with a trowel, big enough so the roots can be spread freely. Water the hole and let it drain a minute or so. Set the plant in the hole at the same depth it was in the container, spreading out its roots. Dribble the soil in, gently firming it around the roots to insure complete contact, until the hole is filled and level with the ground surface. Then water. A light, fine, even mist with a hose is best. Leave the hose turned on until the soil is saturated.

PLANTING SEEDS OUTDOORS: It's a cinch compared to the foregoing. Prepare ground so that the soil is fine and reasonably free from sticks and stones and the surface is level (unless you're planting on a hillside). If you are sowing in rows, you can use your hose as a guide line. Lay it in position and make a little ditch running down its length. (See the directions on the seed package for recommended depth.) Sow the seeds thinly and cover them with soil and tamp down. (If you're broadcasting the seed, simply loosen the soil surface, sprinkle the seeds, and cover them with soil to the recommended depth. Tamp down.) Set the nozzle of the hose for fog, and soak the soil thoroughly.

Keep the soil damp until the seeds germinate and the plants are well on their way. In the early stages you may have to water daily in dry spells, particularly if there is also a high desiccating wind. And don't forget to thin. Be gap-minded and you'll have good plants; check the seed package for ideal distances-apart. Thinnings of early leaf lettuce make a delicious salad and help mitigate that awful feeling you get from the slaughter of helpless little plants.

If you can remember the following, most of the questions that might crop up about soil, planting, and transplanting will automatically be answered.

The soil: Without organic content no soil is fertile. Only in decomposing organic matter can multitudes of bacteria thrive, which in turn yield the organic acids necessary to dissolve minerals and make them useful to plants. Minerals in a soil poor in organic matter are useless to roots and therefore might just as well not be there as far as the plant is concerned. Indeed, a soil lacking in organic matter will usually have a correspondingly much higher mineral content than one rich in organic matter. Feeding mineral fertilizers to such a soil is like feeding salt water to the ocean.

Organic matter should be present in various stages of decomposition, ranging from thoroughly decomposed humus (real humus is like a black jelly) to semi-decomposed peat moss, leaf molds, etc. The former makes nutrients immediately available; the latter, through its subsequent decomposition, acts as a kind of storehouse for plant food. Since the process of decomposition is constantly going on, you'll obviously have to keep adding organic matter to your soil from year to year. Organic mulches which slowly work their way into the soil can relieve you of most of the work.

Air—more specifically, nitrogen and oxygen—is vital to the life of bacteria and plants. Organic matter in various shapes and sizes fluffs and aerates the soil better than organic matter of a homogeneous, fine consistency. Sand, small sticks, pebbles, and other particles which permit air to enter and circulate through the soil are also useful in a dense heavy soil.

Planting and Transplanting: The terms are often confusing to beginners. Planting refers to the physical act of putting a plant into the ground and covering its roots with soil. Transplanting refers to the lifting of a plant from one place, transferring it to another, and *then* planting it. In a sense, with

33. FEEDER ROOTS

the exception of seeds, every plant is a transplant. But there's a big difference between the transplanting of nursery stock to your garden and the transplanting of a plant growing in your garden to another spot; or the transplanting of a plant growing wild.

Although roots always grow down, they also grow every which way in their search for water, the root system spreading in an ever-widening circumference, as circles when a pebble is dropped in water. But as the roots grow, they change in structure and function. The older roots turn into a kind of elaborate branched and rebranched pipe system whose function it is to pass water along while keeping the plant anchored to the ground. Only the last inch of the new-growing tip retains the ability to take in food and water. These "feeder" roots (see picture 33), fine and threadlike to the naked eye, resemble a baby-bottle brush under a magnifying glass. Each hair is seldom more than 1/200 inch thick and ¼ inch long. Tear them off the plant (you can't help it when you transplant), and you cut off a vital food and water supply. But not for long. Pretty soon, new roots burst forth in even greater number to try to make up for the loss. But only if the plant has been able to survive on its reduced rations! How *much* reduced is the problem.

A good nursery is aware of this and will systematically prune roots to restrict the root system to a small area so that the plant may be lifted and transplanted with most of its roots intact. (Plants grown in pots will have almost their entire root system intact, obviously. But not all potted plants are *grown* in pots. They may be last-minute transplants.)

In nature or in your garden, roots are not restricted. In digging up a plant the feeding system may be so severely disrupted that the plant will not be able to survive the period it must wait for new roots to grow. That's why the older the plant to be transplanted, the more important it is to take as much soil with it as you can. This is almost impossible with even a fair-sized tree, as the ball of earth would be so large it would be unmanageable. Beware of tree bargains unless you know the people with whom you're dealing. You may be buying wild trees dug up in the woods. And the root ball may contain nothing but a stump that time will shortly put out of its misery. You might be able to rescue it by cutting back severely—to just a couple of feet—but then, of course, it will take years to grow back.

The function of the feeder roots is to take in water with dissolved minerals and pass them along to the leaf. The leaf, in the presence of light, and only in the presence of light, will combine these elements with gases in the air to form sugars and then starches. Some of this food will be used by the plant for growth, some will be stored in the stems and roots to tide the plant over the winter and to initiate the next year's growth.

In other words, it is the leaf and the leaf alone that can manufacture food, mainly sugar. Roots only serve to supply some of the ingredients needed. The sweetness of the grape, the size, the condition, and the health of the next year's leaves and flowers depend on leaves. The more healthy and abundant the leaves, the more sugar is produced, the more can be stored. This is why you don't remove the leaves to let the sun "sweeten" the tomatoes and you don't cut down the foliage of bulbs after they've flowered.

When growth begins in spring and before the leaves appear, the plant must draw on last season's food storage. By the time it's used up, leaves will have appeared to take over the feeding function. But most of the sugar produced is consumed in active growth. By summer growth has slowed and there's sugar production to spare. That's when sugar is stored and the cycle begins all over again. Therefore, you can see that the condition of your plants one year depends largely on the sugar production of the leaves the year before, which in turn depends on the sun and on water and minerals from the roots.

The leaf, however, doesn't use all the water supplied to it from the roots. Some of it escapes in the form of water vapor . . . called *transpiration*, but *evaporation* will do for our discussion.

Back to what happens with transplanting. Feeder roots are torn. Water intake is sharply reduced. But leaves continue to give off water. If they give it off faster than roots can supply it, wilting occurs. And if new roots don't grow fast enough, wilting gets progressively worse until the plant dies.

What can you do? Several things:

1. Encourage the growth of new roots by placing the existing root system in firm contact with a well-aerated, humusy, moisture-retaining soil medium. Notice—oxygen *and* water—both are necessary. This is why you shouldn't keep plants sopping wet, thereby forcing out all air. And humus contains Vitamin B, the quickest starter for new roots.

2. Reduce evaporation by: shading the plants from the sun; protecting them from strong winds; misting their leaves with a hose (several times during the day, if necessary) to keep them moist; cutting the plant back (the fewer the leaves, the smaller the loss of moisture). If the plant is in dire distress you'll have to prune severely—all the way, back to at least an inch of green wood. You can't always shade or protect plants from winds but you can always spray and cut them back. Most of all, try to plant a robust specimen that was grown in good soil and ample sun the year before.

The larger, the more mature the plant that is to be transplanted, the more attention you have to pay to these things. Even with nursery stock it's well worth your trouble to dig a hole a great deal larger than the root ball and to place substantial sand and humus beneath and around the roots of trees and shrubs. Then there'll be plenty of Vitamin B and oxygen to stimulate new growth plus a ready supply of food once growth has begun.

Evergreens especially, whose roots are always growing, whose leaves are always giving off moisture, should have well-aerated soil near the root ball and have their leaves sprayed when necessary. So should deciduous trees transplanted during their growing period, when they are budding or with leaves on them. If they are planted dormant, bare-root, they are, of course, asleep to it all (obviously the ideal time to plant them), but when their roots start to grow, they'll appreciate your thoughtfulness. Incidentally, when you buy evergreens, always check that the burlapped ball is intact and thoroughly moist, for irreparable damage may be done if they're allowed to dry out at any stage. With some, even a few minutes is critical.

Propagation: Division, Offsets, Cuttings, Ground Layering

Besides seeds there is a variety of ways plants can be made to produce new plants. Forget rules and complicated terms and look at the plant. Does it grow from a bulb or something like a bulb? That is, does it have a thick fleshy root of some kind? Some are really underground stems but it doesn't really matter for our purposes. Although, technically, this group breaks down into categories such as rhizomes, tubers, corms, crowns, bulbs, and all have distinct methods of reproduction, a look at any one will tell you that they reproduce by either division or separation. (Individual requirements are given in the specific plant entries in this book.)

Dig up the plant at the end of the growing season; you'll find the clue to its method of reproduction. Many bulbs, corms, tubers will have produced young bulblets, cormlets, or tubercles, respectively, close to themselves. (They are often called offsets.) All you need to do is pull them apart from their parent and plant them. If there are no noticeable young offspring obviously demanding to be separated, look for "eyes" growing on the fleshy "roots." Simply divide by breaking or cutting into chunks, making sure that each chunk has one or more eyes. From each eye, new leaves or stems will grow.

You can speed up the production of bulblets on some bulbs. Those that grow scales, as some lilies do, can have their loose, outer scales separated and planted to form new bulbs. Or you can simply leave them in the ground and they'll do it by themselves. Some bulbous plants grow bulbils (secondary bulbs) in their leaf axils (the place where leaf grows from twig) or in their flower clusters in plain sight for you to see. Remove, separate, and plant them if you want more plants. Almost-bulbs (crowns) like lily-of-the-valley grow buds (pips) at the base of the stem. Separate and plant them.

Almost everyone knows how to do these things, but some people don't know that many of the hardy "bulbs" (I use the word to cover the whole category of fleshy perennials) need a period of cold storage before growth can begin. Lilies of the valley won't sprout unless they have been frozen for several weeks; crocuses and tulips have to be chilled before they will. Warm-climate gardeners will have to depend on the deepfreeze or refrigerator.

Conversely, tender bulbs like gladioli (corm) and dahlias (tuber) cannot stand freezing, and Northern gardeners will have to lift them out and store them indoors over the winter. Whether a plant is hardy, semihardy, or tender is given under each plant in the dictionary section. No tender bulb can survive freezing; semihardy ones sometimes can if well-mulched; and some hardy bulbs may not have to be refrigerated but it is a common cause of failure in warm climates if they aren't. If in doubt, ask your local dealer.

Plants that have no fleshy roots can also be divided or separated. Again it's easy to see how by looking at the plant. Old plants often grow young plants on their roots (offsets, again). You can see them sprouting up, from, and around the base of the parent plant. Dig to the root system and separate them, being sure to get a piece of root with each stem. Sometimes they can simply be pulled apart, gently does it; sometimes you'll have to cut into the root of the parent. Just be sure to get a piece of root in any case. Many herbaceous (nonwoody) perennials grow plants on their roots; so do many shrubs—check your lilac and see.

If the plant doesn't seem to have young sprouts, you can still divide it. In this case, lift the whole root clump and cut, break, or saw the root mass in half with each half retaining its stems. Plant. Herbaceous perennials can usually be broken or pulled apart; shrub clumps may take chopping or sawing.

Sometimes a plant produces "runners" from which new plants will grow. You'll suddenly notice a young plant growing several feet away from the parent. The runner may be underground or on the top of the ground. If it's underground, just dig gently until you find the runner, then cut and lift the young plant, root and all, for transplanting. If it's on top of the ground, check that the offspring has rooted before you separate it. If it hasn't, you can hasten the process by pinning the runner to the ground where you want it to root. Hairpins and bobby pins are fine for this.

You can also get a plant that doesn't produce runners to grow roots by the following ground-layering system. Bend the branch to the ground, bury it a few inches deep at the point you want it to root, and pin or peg it down. Cover it with soil. The branch will root where it is buried. (You can make it root faster by cutting into the stem a bit. Wedge it open with a pebble.) Some plants do this automatically, weeping forsythia, for example, by arching their tips to the ground. But be sure that stems and leaves are upright: remember, leaves need sun and air to make food.

Not so obvious, but just as effective, is the propagation of plants by cuttings. This can be done with stems, or with leaves (roots, too, but since you won't be doing it, we'll forget them). Just which works best depends on the plant. Some plants root easily from stems or leaves; some are more difficult and take longer; some take ages and are so difficult to root that it is not worth the effort.

34. CUTTINGS ROOTING IN WATER

35. CUTTINGS ROOTED IN WATER

You're probably already familiar with the easy ones. Take a piece of willow, or English ivy, patience, or wax begonia and put it in water (see pictures 34 and 35). In no time at all you'll have roots. All books will tell you that only a few plants will root in water but you'd be surprised at how many I've succeeded in rooting that way. This is not because I want to outsmart anybody but just because I'm busy and somehow it's so simple to fill a glass of water and plunk cuttings into it. At present, I have a six-foot branch of willow, which had to be pruned since it was obstructing the road, with three arching branches growing in a tall glass jug, the kind used for kerosene stoves. The long white roots look lovely, seen through water, particularly when the sun strikes them. Until last week the branches were full of new leaves and buds. Then the parakeets defoliated them completely and now each branch is a long arch with sprays of lavender wisteria in full bloom. Artificial, of course, but they fool everybody.

Willows root easily at any time. But I also root gardenias, flowering maples, bougainvilleas, and hibiscus in water without any trouble . . . just patience. The main reason for failure is the lack of oxygen. I get around this by keeping the water level low in the container once roots have sprouted. This way they get more oxygen—I think! Anyway, they grow.

If you don't want to take chances, grow your cuttings in a medium of half sand and half peat. Note that cuttings rooted in a solid medium grow thicker, chunkier roots, as shown below. Although you can root leaves (even hyacinth and lily leaves will grow "roots"), the most common cuttings for the outdoor garden will be from stems. (If you want to make leaf cuttings, insert the leaf stem in the mix, and follow directions for stem cuttings given below.)

36. CUTTINGS ROOTED IN SOIL MEDIUM

Stem cuttings break down into two types that you've probably heard about: softwood and hardwood. Forget the hardwood cuttings—they're mainly used by commercial growers. Softwood cuttings are all you're interested in. Cut a piece of stem of half-mature growth anywhere from three to eight inches long. Spring or summer is a good time to cut, but the best time varies with the plant. If the growth is too young, it will be too soft and the cutting may rot; if too old, it may be past the ideal rooting time. Here, only experience can guide you. But don't let that stop you. Take a chance and the chances are you'll succeed.

At this point your knowledge of what happens with roots and leaves will stand you in good stead. Here, there are no roots but the leaves continue to give off moisture. Remove some, keep some, and with some broad-leafed plants which give off water over a large area, cut off a piece of leaf tip. Be sure to keep some leaves—or no food manufacture!

Planting cuttings is simple. It is very much like planting seeds indoors. Fill a container with mixture. A flowerpot with a chunk of broken flowerpot covering the hole is the easiest. Soak the mixture with water. Remove all the bottom leaves and insert the cutting firmly into the medium to about half its length. If you haven't already done so, remove more leaves from the stem, leaving but three or four on a short cutting, or five or six on a longer cutting, and then cut a piece off of each leaf if the leaves are very broad. Sprinkle with water to settle the mixture, if necessary.

37. GLASS JAR PROTECTING CUTTINGS

Now to get the cuttings to root! An always damp soil, humidity around leaves, warmth, good light but protection from hot sun are necessary. A glass jar inverted over the pot is of enormous help (see picture 37). It will both reduce evaporation from the leaves and ground and you won't have to water as much or spray the leaves. If you don't use a jar, spray the leaves occasionally and feel the soil daily to make sure it doesn't dry out. Keep the plant out of direct sunlight until new leaves appear. When they do, move the plant to its proper location, a sunny or semishady spot, according to individual plant needs, and *remove the cover.*

The time for rooting varies greatly with each plant. The way to tell is to lift one out and see. If the roots are plentiful and at least an inch or more long, they're ready for transplanting. If not, ease them back into the soil mixture. When you transplant, treat the plant like a seedling, that is, harden it off for a few days outdoors before setting it in ground.

Plant Care

This is usually referred to as "maintenance," an ominous word meaning the relentless upkeep of flower beds, lawns, and foundation plantings of trees and shrubs. I've already indicated how you can avoid that and have a garden instead of gardening. Caring for plants in this sense involves little more than general housekeeping—a little tidying and sprucing up from time to time.

Mulch plants—the deeper the mulch, the fewer weeds, the less evaporation, and the less you'll have to water. However, should you hit a long dry spell and you have to water, then *soak thoroughly.* A few minutes of standing and sprinkling with hose in hand is not the way. At best you may only be soaking the mulch. Or you may be soaking only the first inch or so of ground and thus encouraging shallow roots that won't be able to withstand the next dry spell.

Most people don't realize how long it takes to really soak the ground to a depth of say four or five feet. Turn the sprinkler on, leave it running for several hours in one spot, then move it to another until all the ground has been covered. This is ideal since the spray also washes off leaves. Hoses with little holes punched every two inches are also excellent. But if you are suddenly called away for the day and can't keep changing hose position every two hours, you can use my irrigation system. I simply turn on the hose—a regular hose or one with holes in it—just enough for water to seep, lay it on the ground and go away. Whenever I return, I move it to another spot and continue in this fashion until the area is soaked. Of course, this can take a week (and often does) but you don't have to keep watching it all the time or worry about floods.

From time to time, as you walk about the garden, you'll pick off a few dead leaves, snip off a broken or dead branch, and cut out old dead canes from the center of shrubs. If a shrub or a flower clump gets too big and thick, you'll have to divide it, but this doesn't happen often—and usually you can do it in the spring when you're just dying to get out and do some work anyway. Occasionally, a straggly branch will displease you. Cut it off. A tall, stately plant looks about to topple. Stake it (bamboo stakes sold in gardening centers are attractive). Or you see that a plant is not "bushing" very nicely. Pinch off a few inches of tips at the top and sides. It will branch out from under the pinch. Or that flower buds are growing in too thick clusters. Pinch some out, leaving room for others to grow bigger (disbudding).

You suddenly notice that a tree looks very twiggy and leafless near the bottom. No sun? Make corrections accordingly with judicious pruning. The same goes for thick tangled growth. Cut out some of it and let the sun and air get to the leaves so they can manufacture food. Light pruning, here and there, can also be done to shape or reshape a plant without harm. Heavy, drastic pruning, however, is best left to experts.

You'll also notice bugs and insects and various other ills! What to do? Well, I'll tell you one thing I *don't* do is to get out those toxic sprays which indiscriminately destroy bad and good insects, poison the birds that eat the insects, and are washed into the ground with the next rain to destroy all the bacteria that make my soil fertile.

I think by now enough has been written for everyone to realize how exceedingly harmful and useless insecticides are—to the ground; to the plant; to the birds (entire species are in dire danger of extinction); to the fish in the seas where the poisoned waters drain; and last but not least to man himself. Besides, insecticides produce more destructive, insecticide-resistant types. If you haven't already heard and read about this in the papers, let me refer you to the book of that eminent biologist, Rachel Carson's *Silent Spring*, and you'll never again have an insecticide, or many of those other lethal sprays in pretty cans we're all used to keeping around the house. Don't let anybody fool you that there's a safe and unsafe way to use them. Any amount of DDT stored in fat tissue—and every woman, man, and child in America has it from the milk, meat, butter, vegetables, and fruits he eats—is just that much too much DDT for me.

Besides, before I knew all that I know now of their danger, I never found insecticides to work any better than just leaving things be. I sprayed for birchleaf miners once when I was told by two authorities that unless I did I would lose the trees. It was a ghastly experience involving expensive equipment, the complicated covering of adjacent plants, my entire body, and not breathing during the whole process. The tree did survive. Some leaves were bloated with miners, some not. Some fell off, new ones grew. The following year I did nothing and haven't since. The results were identical.

Another episode: Oaks in the community suddenly developed anthracnose. Big trees, big job of spraying. Some people had it done at fifty dollars a tree. I didn't. What happened? All our trees lost their leaves and then grew new ones. The next year all the trees had healthy leaves.

Another episode: One season the gnats in the community were particularly bad. An entire tree-spraying program was ordered. Trees, gnats, birds, children, dogs, cats were thoroughly sprayed. What happened? I stayed indoors, but the cat didn't. He got violently ill and the birds almost completely "disappeared." The following year, I noticed that the robins acted most peculiarly, setting and setting on eggs that never hatched. I couldn't understand it then.

So what do you do . . . just allow your plants to be killed? Well, in the first place, they most likely won't be killed or even seriously injured. If you've grown a plant well, with good soil, ample light and water, it can survive most marauders without help. But help it has without help from you. Most insects have their own individual foes—your friends. Encourage friends. Birds obviously—running water, or bird bath—that's all you need to attract them. And don't go around indiscriminately slaughtering any bug that looks mean to you unless you know which bug feeds on your plants and which feeds on those that feed on your plants. You may, indeed, somewhere along the line, lose a plant (I still never have). Maybe two, maybe more. So what? You can always get another. It's not the end of the world. The other way could prove to be!

If you're not squeamish you can help nature along. When rosebuds show a cluster of little bugs I squash them off. Ditto with little cottony mealybug clusters in leaf axils. Caterpillarlike creatures are happily gathered by young children and squashed (I feed mine to our chameleon). Japanese beetles? They're no real problem. Keep a little tin can with kerosene handy and plop them into it whenever you see one or the mood strikes you. Diseased leaves and other tissue I simply keep picked off and throw in the garbage pail or burn in the fireplace. If I happen to have a plant which insists on making itself unattractive —one rose I had could not be coaxed to give up its powdery mildew, even when I kept it dry and gave it more sun—I get rid of it. There are plenty of plants that aren't so unobliging!

Above all, don't worry about making mistakes in gardening. There is no one way to do anything. No book or books, no advice can match trial and error. Just do things your way. You'll be surprised how often it works.

38.

FREE LABOR. Earthworms till the soil for you, "eating" earth from below, bringing their useful castings to the surface, and then carrying down humus and leaf mold into the soil again. They can only live and breed in rich humusy soil, but there they thrive—at the rate of a quarter million to the quarter acre. Of course, if you spray your plants with poisons, the poisons will eventually work down in the soil, killing your earthworms. Then you'll have to do all the work yourself!

Plants for the Home Garden

Below are explanations of terms used in the text which may not be familiar to you:

ANNUALS: Plants which grow from seed, bloom, set seed, and perish, all within the same season. They are often mistaken for perennials since they seed themselves and thus come up the following year. (Only hardy seeds can do this in Northern climates.) Conversely some tender perennials, which under the right conditions will produce bloom the first year and then are killed in the winter by freezing, are treated and listed as annuals in catalogs.

BEDDING PLANTS: Tender perennials, such as geraniums, grown in pots for planting outdoors in Northern summers. They should be lifted and brought indoors in fall.

BIENNIALS: Plants which live for only two seasons. Usually planted from seed, they generally grow leaves the first season and flowers the second, before they die. However, the lines are not always so clearly drawn. Some biennials are semiperennial in habit and persist into a third season; some will bloom the first year, if given a long growing season.

DECIDUOUS: The common and botanical term applied to trees, shrubs, and other woody plants that shed their leaves annually. There is great variation according to the plant and the climate. *(See Evergreen below.)*

EVERGREEN: Shrubs, trees, and other plants that do not shed their leaves annually, but retain their foliage from year to year. There is great variation according to plant, climate, and region. Some plants are evergreen in mild climates and deciduous in the North; most plants are evergreen in the tropics. Rainy and dry seasons also affect leaf retention—some evergreens in mild climates become deciduous in dry seasons. Usually "evergreen" is applied to only shrubs and trees and woody plants. A semievergreen is a plant that has semipersistent foliage even in cold regions.

GROUND COVERS: Dwarf plants used to carpet the ground in shady or difficult places. They usually spread by creeping and rooting in all directions, creating a solid ever-expanding plant mass; or by long trailers or runners which root and form new plants. Evergreens are the most desirable.

HARDY: Used here in the popular sense to mean a plant that will survive freezing temperatures.

HEDGES: Shrubs or trees that can be grown in close proximity and can withstand constant shearing. Not all can. With those that do, careful attention must be paid to see that lower branches receive sun lest defoliation take place. The shape of hedges should always be wide at the bottom, narrowing to the top. They require constant pruning or they may lose their shape forever. For busy people, attractive fencing combined with plants is recommended.

PANICLE: Individual flowers massed in long, loose clusters of various shapes and sizes, such as lilac.

PERENNIALS: Plants that live and flower year after year. The word is used here in its popular sense to mean herbaceous perennials, nonwoody plants, not shrubs and trees. Perennials vary widely in their degree of persistence, some producing satisfactory blooms for only three seasons while others live on for a very long time. Perennials listed here include the fleshy-rooted perennials, such as bulbs, rhizomes, corms, and tubers.

RACEME: A long flower cluster of individual flowers on short stalks individually strung on a main flower stalk, such as lily-of-the-valley.

ROCK GARDEN PLANTS: The name is used not to suggest the planning of rock gardens but only to include plants that will grow in stony locations exposed to sun and wind. These plants are naturally dwarf, persistent in relatively infertile soil, and interesting for flower, fruit, foliage, or shape. Some grow erect, like miniature "garden" perennials; some creep, rooting as they go to fill crevices; some grow in low rosettes which multiply to spread over a given area.

SEMIHARDY: Used in the popular sense to mean a plant which will stand some frost if protected—by mulch or some other covering which allows air to enter.

TENDER: Plants that tolerate no frost.

Perennials and Biennials

AMARYLLIS (*Hippeastrum: also see Hardy Amaryllis under Perennials and Biennials*). Tender perennial, one of the showiest plants for middle and deep South, California, the Gulf states; excellent summer-blooming bulb for the North. Giant lilylike

1. AMARYLLIS

blooms to 10 inches across, borne 2 to 3 to a stalk from bulb which often sends up several stalks. Wide ranges of colors from pale pink to orange, apricots, salmon to red to purples, pure white and variegated forms. Long lasting, but does not like to be moved. CULTURE: Sun, rich, well-drained soil, and plenty of water during growing season. If grown as summer bulb in the North, it can be set quite early in the garden as it needs a long growing period. Leave bulbs in the ground until light frost nips them, then dig up, dry, and store in sand. A favorite pot plant. Failure to bloom is often due to plant being allowed to become too dry before foliage ripens. PROPAGATION: Offsets.

ASTILBE; SPIREA (*Astilbe*). Graceful, upright, bushy plants with fernlike foliage and feathery panicles of bloom in very pretty shades of white, pink, rose, red, purple, some bicolored rose-pink, and dark blue. Many good hardy species and varieties. Height from 2 to 6 feet. Plants start blooming in early summer and continue for long period (July to September) under proper conditions (plenty of water). *A. Arendsii* hybrids to 3 feet are among the best for garden culture. CULTURE: Partial shade, easy to grow in rich, moist soil. PROPAGATION: Division of clumps every 3 years or so in early spring or immediately after flowering; seed.

2. ASTILBE

BALLOON FLOWER; CHINESE BELL FLOWER (*Platycodon grandiflorum*). Very handsome bushy plant to 2 to 3 feet or more, with waxen, balloon-shaped buds that open into large flowers 3 inches across. Single or double in sky-blues, purplish blues, white, pinks. Also some dwarf species that grow to about 12 inches high. Foliage is unusually handsome, deeply toothed, dark glossy green. Bloom July and August; winter hardy. CULTURE: Sun, will tolerate a little shade (fewer blooms but more pungent color). Any good well-drained soil. PROPAGATION: Easy from seed, or by division in the spring.

3. BALLOON FLOWER

BEARD-TONGUE (*Penstemon*). A misnomer if there ever was one, conjuring up nothing descriptive about these panicles of graceful bell-like brilliantly colored florets. Many colors, many varieties from evergreen creepers to tall shrublike types. Colors: white, shell pinks, corals, beautiful range of blues, including shimmering purple or crimson. **Giant Floradale,** shown here, has flower spikes to 3 feet with long, tubular, brilliant blooms, some daintily edged. Some 125 species, many with long summer blooming period. CULTURE: Full sun, easy

4. BEARD-TONGUE (Giant Floradale)

to grow, will tolerate dryness; winter hardy. Rewarding to grow from seed with fall plantings preferred. PROPAGATION: Seed; cuttings taken in summer.

BLAZING STAR; GAY FEATHER (*Liatris*). Tall erect spikes (3 to 6 feet depending on species), solidly covered from top to bottom with fluffy blossoms in bright purple, rose purple, rose, or white. Robust, winter hardy, of easy culture, these plants bloom from the tops down from midsummer until autumn. Very attractive to bees and butterflies too. CULTURE: Sun or shade, average soil. PROPAGATION: Seed, in fall; division of clumps or tuberous roots.

5. BLAZING STAR

BLEEDING HEART (*Dicentra spectabilis*). An old-fashioned graceful favorite with arching sprays of drooping rosy, heart-shaped blossoms; fernlike foliage. One of the first nonbulbous flowers to bloom, heralding spring along with tulips and late narcissi (April to June). It has the added attribute of flowering in shade. Grows to 2 feet. *D. formosa alba* grows to 1 foot, has very beautiful white flowers as everblooming **Sweetheart** shown here (good for West Coast). CULTURE: Sun or light shade—will tolerate fairly deep shade; rich "humusy," moist, well-drained soil. PROPAGATION: Cutting of fleshy roots. Winter hardy in very cold climates. Other good *Dicentra* are: **Dutchmans Breeches** (*D. Cucullaria*)

6. BLEEDING HEART (Sweetheart)

with flowers white, tipped yellow; to 10 inches; good for naturalizing or rock garden. **Fringed Bleeding Heart;** 1 to 2 feet; delicate fernlike foliage; rosy flowers; good for naturalizing or rock garden; long blooming season.

CALADIUM (*Caladium bicolor*). Generally listed as "Fancy-Leaved," which indeed they are; large, handsome, superbly variegated, mottled, veined, and margined in green and white, red and white, red and

7. CALADIUM

pinks. Grown from tubers (usually called bulbs); not hardy in the North. CULTURE: Sun recommended for reds, shade for pinks and whites. Rich, moist, peaty soil helps bring out true colors. In mild climates tubers may be planted at any frost-free time, 1 to 2 inches deep, 6 inches apart (do not worry if they are planted upside down). After foliage dies down, dig up and dry, store in cool, dry place. Tubers may be replanted in a month or so or held over to the following year. In cold climates, start tubers indoors in pots (½ inch deep in wet peat) in early spring, 1 tuber per 5-inch pot. Transplant when all danger of frost is over. Dig up before frost and store over winter. PROPAGATION: Division. Make a very satisfactory house plant during the winter but should be given a month's "curing" time before replanting.

CALLA LILY (*Zantedeschia*). Tender perennial grown from thick rhizomes. Handsome plants with large, elegant,

8. GOLDEN CALLA LILY

trumpet-shaped blossoms; arrow-shaped leaves. **Golden Calla** (*Z. Elliottiana*), shown here, has golden-yellow blooms, green leaves spotted white, 1½ to 2 feet; has been reported as surviving below zero in Piedmont, Virginia. **Common Calla** (*Z. aethiopica*) is white; **Red Calla** (*Z. Rehmannii*) is pink-red; **Black Calla** (*Arum palaestinum*) is purplish-black; the **Spotted Calla** (*albo-maculata*) is a purple-throated cream. Most cultivated species hardy to about middle South. In the North plants may be grown in pots, set outdoors for the summer, and lifted in the fall to be given a rest period. (Lay pot on its side in cool dry place for about 3 months.) CULTURE: Light shade, rich, "humusy," moist soil, but well drained. Plant 1 inch deep. PROPAGATION: Offsets from bulbs. The **Golden Calla** may be rather easily propagated from seed.

CANTERBURY BELLS (*Campanula medium*). The only thing wrong with these is that they are biennial, blooming only the

9. CANTERBURY BELLS

second year from seed (although there are some that will bloom the first year if started early indoors). Part of a large genus of some of the most graceful plants known. Singles are typically bell-shaped as shown here with large rose, white, or blue flowers (3 feet). Doubles have a bell within a bell, very floriferous (2 to 2½ feet). A great favorite are the **Cup-and-Saucers Bells** (*C. Medium calycanthema*) in lovely shades of dark blue, white, and rose and lilac. All are June bloomers. The hardy perennial Campanulas are the **Bellflowers**—much varied in shape and habits of growth. Some of the best listed are: **Carpathian Bellflower** (*C. Carpatica: see Rock Gardens*). **Peach Bells** (*C. persicifolia*)—Large, handsome, bell-shaped flowers, singles and doubles; white or many shades of blue on erect stiffish stalks, usually unbranched, 2 to 3 feet. Bloom June to August. ***C. lactiflora***—Tall, leafy 3- to 5-foot stems with terminal panicles of star-shaped bells in pale blue or milk white. Bloom July and August. **Royal Bellflower** (*C. latifolia*)—Handsome, stately spikes (3 to 4 feet) of funnel-shaped flowers in blue, purplish blue, white; blooms June through August. ***C. latiloba*** (*C. grandis*)—Large bell- to saucer-shaped flowers solitary or clustered on 1- to 2-foot stems, in pale or deep blue; blooms June through August. CULTURE: Part shade, any good well-drained soil. Start seeds in May or June for following year's bloom. Easy to transplant even when in bloom.

CARNATIONS (*Dianthus caryophyllus: see Pinks, Sweet William under Perennials*). Much admired but much neglected plant in this country, usually relegated to the florist,

10. CARNATION (Red Wonder)

perhaps because it is little known that there are such excellent hardy garden types, both biennial and perennial. **Red Wonder,** shown here, has heavily-fringed, highly perfumed, 3-inch pure red flowers which bloom profusely on upright stems 18 to 20 inches long. There are many listed strains including dwarf types, in a range of red, scarlet, white, and yellow; also bicolored, varicolored in both delicate and brilliant hues of cream, coral, orange; grayed lavenders, purple, fuchsia, and cherry—all are characteristically scented. There is also the annual **Marguerite**—carnations that bloom from seed the first year (allow 5 months), often blooming again the following year except in severe climates; these are equally showy and fragrant (15 to 18 inches tall). CULTURE: Sun, well-drained soil, with an extra helping of lime if soil is acid. If seed sown early many will bloom the same season. Cut stalks immediately after blooming. Perennials may be cut back in the fall, and potted for indoor winter bloom. PROPAGATION: Seed; cuttings.

CHRYSANTHEMUM (*Chrysanthemum*). Species and varieties are so numerous that any attempt to list them would fill a book. **Shasta Daisies, Pyrethrum, Painted Daisy, Ox-Eye-Daisy, Feverfew, Marguerites** or **Paris Daisy** are all Chrysanthemums (but not all are winter hardy). And that's just the beginning! Modern Chrysanthemums are so constantly hybridized that even 5-year-old varieties are considered outdated. In fact, 11 new garden mums were "Jury-approved" only during 1961. Whatever its name or heritage, none could be fairer for fall blooms, nor more prolific, nor easier to grow. And the variety and color are almost limitless—button types or pompon, aster-like, dwarf or large flowering. Following are colors of the eleven new (1961) Jury-approved mums—all winter hardy: **Stern's Sunbeam,** shown here, has spectacular blooms starting in early August; strong, clear yellow flowers 4 to 5 inches across without disbudding; 5 to 6 inches with disbudding. **Raspberry Festival**—Rose with silvery lilac overcast recurved petals; 3 inches across. **Purple Finch**—Cerise red-purple with silvery reverse; to 6 inches wide. **Jack Frost**—Pure white opening from shell pink bud; 3 inches wide. **Hummingbird**—Soft, clean, clear, pink to 6½ inches wide—graceful, shaggy. **Song Sparrow**—Rich sandy pastel, opening from bright orange through peach-colored buds; 6½

11. CHRYSANTHEMUM (Stern's Sunbeam)

inches wide. **Bingo**—Brilliant crimson cushion-type mums in sprays up to 2½ inches wide. **Apricot Sheen**—Golden peach apricot, mounds of double cushion-type flowers to 2½ inches wide. **Chestnut Warbler**—Scarlet bronze with gold bronze reverse to 6½ inches wide. **Her Majesty**—Ivory with petals barely pink-suffused to 3 inches wide; in sprays. **Streamlined**—Taupey pastel walnut with tiny mahogany eye; button-pompon to 1 inch wide. CULTURE: Full sun for good bloom, a little shade tolerated; good rich soil; plenty of moisture during growing season. Pinching and disbudding common to promote branching and large blooms; pinch off tips when plants are 6 inches high; again when about 10 inches high. Tall varieties need staking. PROPAGATION: Division of clumps—best to do each spring for better blooms (discard center woody portion). Plant 12 to 18 inches apart depending on variety. Also from seed.

COLUMBINE (*Aquilegia*). Large, graceful spurred flowers borne on slender stalks 1 to 4 feet in height. Many species and varieties in a wide color range, pastels as well as pungent tones, pale blue to purple, white, rose and reds, yellows and bicolors. Pri-

12. McKANA'S GIANT COLUMBINE

marily early summer bloomers, although some flower into late summer. Very hardy —they adapt well to all but southernmost climates. **McKana's Giant Columbine** (All-American Bronze Medal Winner), shown here, has flowers about 4 inches across with 3 to 4 wide spurs, in blues, pinks, maroon, purple, red, yellows, and bicolors red and white, and blue and white. To 3 feet. *A. alpina* grows to 1 foot, with blue-violet flowers to 2 inches across; *var. alba* is white. **Fan Columbine** (*A. flabellata*)—To 1½ feet with delicate nodding lilac-blue flowers to 2 inches across. *Var. nana-alba* is one of the best pure whites. **American Columbine** (*A. canadensis*)—To 2½ feet with yellow, red flowers to 2 inches across in May through July. **Golden Columbine** (*A. chrysantha*)—To 3½ feet, much branched lemon yellow, golden yellow, some whites; blooms into late summer (June through August) and is more tolerant of heat and drought. *A. longissima* grows to 3 feet with canary-yellow, long-spurred flowers to 5 inches across. Blooms July through October, and is tolerant of heat and drought. **Colorado Columbine** (*A. caerulea*)—To 3 feet with mauvy, lavender-blue flowers to 2 inches across; blooms May and June; variety *cuprea* is copper red with darker spurs; *rosea* is a rosy pink hybrid; *lutea* is blue or pink with white or yellow; *citrina* is yellow; *alba* and *candissima* are white; and *Heleniae* is blue and white. **European Columbine** (*A. vulgaris*)—To 2½ feet with nodding purple, white, blue flowers, to 2 inches across, which bloom in May. *A. clematiflora* hybrids—To 1½ feet with pale pink and blue flowers to 3 inches across. CULTURE: Plant clumps 12 to 18 inches apart, in sun or light shade; moist rich soil. PROPAGATION: Seed usual. Sow in spring for next spring's blooms. Division, every 5 to 6 years, in spring. Protect from strong winds.

CORAL BELLS (*Heuchera sanguinea*). Gay, graceful little bells strung like tiny jewels on each stem above a tuft of leaves. **Bressingham Hybrids,** shown here, are from palest pink to deepest crimson, and bloom in June. Often found in rocky nooks. There are also white **Coral Bells.** Different species bloom from May until August. All are winter hardy. CULTURE: Sun or light shade such as that in spring woodlands. Average to rich "humusy" soil. PROPAGATION: Seed or division—should be divided or reset every 2 or 3 years.

13. CORAL BELLS (Bressingham Hybrids)

COREOPSIS; TICKSEED (*Coreopsis*). Showy, hardy plants excellent for cutting.

Profuse bloomers for long period (May to Autumn) if not allowed to seed. Both dwarf and tall varieties; from 8 inches to 4 feet high. Daisylike or starlike flowers (½ to 3 inches wide) in the single varieties to fluffy, frilled blooms in double varieties. Flowers borne singly or in branched clusters on strong stems, colors mainly in yellow-orange-red, maroon range. **Golden Wave**

14. COREOPSIS

(*C. grandiflora*), shown here, has double or semidouble bright golden yellow flowers borne on long stiff stems up to 3 feet. Vigorous-growing, drought-resistant. Annual ***Coreopsis,*** usually called ***Calliopsis*** or ***Leptosyne,*** includes some crimsons and is even more drought-tolerant. CULTURE: Full sun, any good soil. PROPAGATION: Easy from seed; division in early spring or fall.

CROCUS (*Crocus*). Hardy cormous perennial, among the first of the hardy spring-flowering "bulbs" to bloom. Cheerful little cups of blue, white, yellow, orange-yellow, light blue, lilac, rose-lilac, bronze, often striped, many large-flowered doubles. Foliage is dark green and grasslike with pale stripes. Many species, some fall blooming such as *C. zonatus,* pale pink to lilac; *C. speciosus,* light blue; *C. ochroleucus,* ivory-tinged apricot; *C. longiflorus,* mauve with yellow throat. One of the most commonly grown Autumn Crocuses, shown here, is *Colchichum autumnale,* a relative of the lily family with crocuslike blooms to 4 inches across. Single or double blooms in white, rose-pink, purple. **Pickwick,** a spring-flowering crocus, is one of the most beautiful striped strains cultivated: large, well-

15. AUTUMN CROCUS

shaped blooms, white with lavender stripes, purple feathering, deep rich purple base, brilliant orange stigma. **Jeanne d'Arc,** also spring flowering, is an outstanding example of the white crocus, and has a pale lavender flush at base. Both very vigorous and floriferous. CULTURE: Sun, well-drained soil; plant corms about 3 inches deep, 2 to 3 inches apart, in early fall for spring bloomers; August for fall bloomer. PROPAGATION: Division; dig up and separate corms every 3 years.

DAFFODILS: A confusing array of mostly hardy spring bulbs variously called **jonquils, daffodils, narcissi.** Apparently the name

16. DAFFODIL (Trumpet)

daffodil has now been decided on to cover the waterfront and a very pretty one it is too, from tiny miniature types to giant modern hybrids with flowers up to 4 inches across. Blooms in early spring; flowers are of various shapes, usually solitary, in yellows varying to cream to white; some with brilliant orange crowns or pinkish trumpets; some doubles with waxy petals; and some bicolors. Species, varieties, and hybrids are legion and worth exploring. Three typical shapes shown here: (1) trumpet type; (2) Narcissus type (at one time this was called *N. incomparabilis Aquila*); and (3) 1960 International Dutch bulb selection **Treviathion,** a jonquil-hybrid-type daffodil with clusters of 2 or 3 fragrant buttercup-yellow flowers. CULTURE: Plant bulbs in September or October in any good soil; sun, part shade, even full shade since they appear before most leaves are out. Bulbs vary in size —plant about 3 times as deep as the total

17. DAFFODIL (Narcissus)

height of bulb. Winter mulch beneficial. Remove withered blooms at the base. Do not remove leaves until they have completely died down. PROPAGATION: Divide every few years for better blooms.

18. DAFFODIL (Treviathion)

DAHLIA (*Dahlia*). These tender tuberous-rooted perennials have come to be tagged the gentlemen's favorite, supposedly because more men than women fancy growing large, showy prize-winning specimens (with blooms up to 14 inches in diameter). There are also more "feminine," small-flowering types with frilled, quilled, or curled petals of single bloom; starlike types; pompon types; very diminutive types; cactus types; orchid-flowering; peony-flowering; in any color or bicolor you can name except blue. Some I find quite garish, others lovely, such as **Lavender Perfection,** shown here, with flawless blooms of lavender-pink. All dahlias are prolific bloomers and easy to grow. CULTURE: Sun and deep, rich, well-drained soil. Plant large-flowering

19. DAHLIA (Lavender Perfection)

types 3 to 4 feet apart. (They will need staking.) Plant small-flowering types 2 feet apart. (Many of these are treated as annuals because they will grow from seed the first season if started early.) Set roots 3 inches deep with eye toward surface of ground. Keep well watered, particularly during hot weather. Tubers are not winter hardy but will come through winters where the ground itself does not freeze. In cold regions, dig up and store dry. PROPAGATION: Division.

DAY LILY (*Hemerocallis*). Just to give you an idea of what has happened to the old orange or yellow Day Lily, here is a list of six new 1961 plants: **Border King**—coral with cherry-red eye, marked yellow throat, 8 to 9 inches across on 4-foot scape. **Green Stripe**—deep orange, extremely recurved blooms; each sepal marked with outer green midrib on 5½- to 6-foot stems. **Night Beat**—clear, light orchid-purple with red eye and yellow throat, up to 4 feet. **Roan**

20. DAY LILY

Beauty—shimmering red brown with deep purple-red eye zone. Wide petaled on 3-foot scrapes. **Royal Coachman**—huge flaring flowers, soft cream yellow with brownish-red eye zone and bright butter-yellow throat; 3 feet high. **Summer Holiday**—large, well-opened flowers of apricot with soft brown eye zone; 3 feet high. Actually everything but pure white and blues have been developed; also many intermediate shades, eyed, banded, and bicolored. One of the easiest plants to grow, with blooms available from June to September depending on the variety. CULTURE: Just about any kind of soil; just about everywhere in the country, drought or wetness, sun or shade. Very robust; actually bloom best with some shade in hot afternoon sun. PROPAGATION: Division—every 3 or 4 years in early spring or after flowering. Shipped at any time, spring through fall, and plantable any time. Set crowns at soil level or slightly below. Seed, but not usual.

DELPHINIUM (*Delphinium*). Unrivaled for color, stateliness, and profusion of blooms. Individually spurred florets, single or double, carried on commanding spikes reaching to 6 feet in the **Pacific Hybrids** shown here. Other good colors now developed—true pinks and reds along with the old fashioned whites, lavenders, dark blues (some double florets combining two distinct shades). There is even a true navy and a yellow. New dwarf variety developed in 1961 (**Blue Tit**) is a striking royal blue, grows to a compact 3 feet with 2 feet of flowering spike. One of the few modern perennials easily grown from seed; extremely winter hardy but apt to languish in warm regions—better adapted to Alaska than the deep South where they are best treated as biennials or annuals. CULTURE: Any good well-drained soil; sunny location preferred but will tolerate some light shade.

21. DELPHINIUM (Pacific Hybrid)

Keep well watered but watch out for crown rot. Keep crown level with surface of ground and do not allow to be covered with soil. Even a winter mulch should not be allowed to pack around crown—use sand or other light, breathing material. Culture is easy from seed sown in July or August for next year's bloom. Chinese types and Giant Pacifics can be sown in early spring for summer bloom and fall bloom respectively. Will often bloom again if flower stalks are cut back after blooming. PROPAGATION: Division of clumps or cuttings from shoots, spring or fall. Easy to transplant in any stage of growth—divide only every 3 or 4 years. In South it is best to order sturdy seedlings from the North and set out in October, or to handle as annual. POPULAR LISTED VARIETIES: ***D. grandiflorum*** (*D. chinense*)—semidwarfs and dwarfs, some known as **Bouquet Larkspur;** bloom July to August; 2 to 3 feet high with 1- to 2-foot sprays of white to gentian blue florets; plant 8 to 12 inches apart. ***D. cheilanthum***—blooms June to July; 3 to 4 feet high; large single flowers, light to turquoise blue in *belladonna*, gentian to dark blue in *bellamosum* (the horticultural varieties of the Chinese type). **Garland Larkspur** belongs to this group. Plant some 12 inches apart. **Garden Hybrids** (*D. elatum-cheilanthum*) —bloom June to July; 4 to 6 feet or more; flowers 2 inches across, frequently double. Leading strain, **Pacific Hybrids,** range from delicate pastels to brightest hues—pinks, mauve-pinks, raspberry, azure, sky-blue, dark blue, white, lavender, purple with many opaline variations, some with brown or black "bees." Bloom June to July; plant 1½ to 2 feet apart.

ENGLISH DAISY (*Bellis perennis*). Even these, the true English daisies, no longer look like daisies, with modern cultivated ones more often double (**Super Enorma,** shown here, has ball-shaped blooms 3 inches across), sometimes with quilled rays. Both types are very pretty, growing out of their low foliage clusters on long stems among Iris and other June blooms. Singles in white or pink with typical yellow eye. Doubles include rose, reds, dark reds, and are often so full as to completely obscure the "eye." Easy to grow; long blooming period; hardy perennials often behaving as biennials. CULTURE: Sow seed in August for next year's bloom. Sun. Under cool moist conditions, will often last more than 2 years; under adverse conditions best to treat as an annual.

22. ENGLISH DAISY (Super Enorma)

FEVERFEW (*Chrysanthemum Parthenium* often listed as *Matricaria parthenoides*). Actually a short-lived perennial, not reliably hardy in the North and best treated as an annual. Will flower from seed first season, frequently seeds itself. Very attractive, floriferous masses of tiny chrysanthemumlike flowers and foliage usually 8 to 10 inches high. Prominent colors available are golden yellows such as **Golden Ball** shown here; lemon yellows (**Lemon Ball**); pure white (**Snowball,** naturally). CULTURE: Easy to grow, prefers sun, but will bloom in semishade.

23. FEVERFEW (Golden Ball)

FOXGLOVE (*Digitalis*). Old-fashioned favorite of considerable dignity with tall, spirelike habit of growth (2 to 6 feet). There are both perennials and biennials, the latter being decidedly the more showy. Prize winner **Excelsior** hybrid, shown here (to 4 feet or more), is a biennial; has gloxinialike flowers tightly massed on freely-blooming spikes. Colors: rose pink, purple, cream, white, shell, prettily marked and spotted. Modern **Giant Shirley** hybrids grow up to 6 feet, have especially large bell-shaped flowers in myriad colors, heavily spotted in red, maroon, chocolate. Other popular foxgloves are: **Yellow Foxgloves** (*D. ambigua*)—perennial or biennial with yellow flowers, blotched brown; 2 to 3 feet. **Grecian Foxglove** (*D. lanata*)—perennial or biennial, numerous flowers the color of sweet butter; to 3 feet. **Rusty Foxglove** (*D. ferruginea*)—perennial or biennial, terracotta red with bearded lower lip; to 6 feet. **Straw Foxglove** (*D. lutea*)—perennial with yellow or white flowers; to 2 feet. ***D. Lutzii*** —biennial hybrids with shades of coral flowers; to 3 feet. CULTURE: Easily grown. They like sun but can stand light shade. Seeds sown in June bloom the following year. Perennials may also be started in late summer. PROPAGATION: Of perennials—division; of biennials—seed.

24. FOXGLOVE (Excelsior)

FREESIA (*Freesia*). This is a plant everybody should grow, for its delicate colors and delicious fragrance are unmatched in the plant kingdom. Clustered, funnellike blooms, very fragrant, exquisitely tinted pink, rose, coral, lilac, blue, yellow, or pure white. Unfortunately freesias cannot stand temperatures below 26 degrees, but they grow indoors very nicely if planted September 15 to December 1 and kept cool and moist in bright sun. Blooms 10 to 12 weeks

25. FREESIA

after planting if temperature is kept in the 50- to 60-degree range. Planted outdoors in mild climates, they will last several years. CULTURE: Sun, cool moist rich soil. Plant corms 3 inches deep. *Indoor culture:* Cover corms with about 1 inch of soil, 6 to 8 corms to an 8-inch pot. Keep moist during active growth. After blooming, gradually reduce and finally withhold water. Store in the pot in a dry place. Repot and repeat procedure next year. PROPAGATION: Division of corms; offsets; seeds.

GERANIUMS (*Geranium, Pelargonium*). To most people in the North geraniums mean the typically white or pink or red tender bedding plant they grow outdoors in summer or in pots in winter (see photo). Technically these are but one of many florist's geraniums of the genus *Pelargonium* —a tender perennial grown rampantly outdoors in mild climates. The true geraniums of the genus *Geranium* are mostly hardy perennials as *Geranium grandiflorum* shown here. Both are members of the *Geraniaceae*

26. GERANIUM (Fairyland)

28. GARDEN GERANIUM (Floradale Fancy)

family. There are many species of both genera, well worth exploring for their lovely flowers or foliage or fragrance and habitual sturdiness. I shall differentiate between them here as follows: **HARDY GERANIUMS.** Sometimes called **Cranesbills,** come in great variety of shapes, sizes, have varied habits of growth. *G. grandiflorum* grows to 1 foot or more, has rosy-blue-lavender flowers veined in purple, 1 inch across. *G. Grevilleanum* is a trailer with soft rose flowers to 2 inches across, often spotted violet. *G. sanguineum* varieties have flowers reddish purple, white, dark magenta, pale rose; some are tall to 1½ feet, others of low compact habit (*nanum*); still others are dwarf (*prostratum*). *G. maculatum* grows to 2 feet, has rose, purple, or white flowers 1 inch across. *G. pratense* grows to 3 feet with lavender-blue or pure white flowers. *G. Endressi* grows to 1½ feet with lovely small pink flowers with rose veining. All of them have attractive foliage, usually deeply cut and well shaped. **TENDER GERANIUMS.** Here the wealth of plants is beyond listing. In general there are four main categories. Most commonly grown are: The Garden Geraniums—typically the one shown here (**Floradale Fancy**) is possibly the best known, but I include a photo of **Apple**

27. GERANIUM GRANDIFLORUM

29. GARDEN GERANIUM (Apple Blossom Rosebud)

Blossom Rosebud just to give you an idea of what you may be missing. There are singles, doubles, carnation-flowered, miniature rosebud-flowered, cactus-flowered, dwarf, medium, tall, in many subtle shadings and mixtures of hues—vivid red, bright pink, white, coral, pink, pale lilac, salmon pink, salmon orange, cerise red, pinky white, orchid pink, purple crimson, violet purple, dark red, scarlet apricot, orange red, cerise. The Ivy Geraniums—floriferous trailers or climbers often substituted for ivy in warm climates. These have very glossy green or variegated leaves, looser umbels of flowers in white to rose, carmine and lavenders. Scented Leaf Geraniums—mostly prized for their fragrance—again a large group with pungent, lacy, and cut ornamental foliage that smells of lemon, rose, peppermint, apple, strawberry, nutmeg, etc. Here the flowers, although pretty, are secondary to the leaves. The Fancy Leaf Geraniums—include the **Lady Washington** type, with large pink, white, or red flowers; and myriad others with foliage variegated green-white, bronze-gold, red, copper, yellow, silver ivory or white markings; sometimes tricolored. Greens alone range from deep, rich and dark to light and airy. Textures from smooth and glossy to petal-soft and velvety. Flowers are single or double in typical color range. Anyone interested in geraniums should certainly avail themselves of dealers' catalogs. CULTURE: Full sun in the North; light shade in hot climates. Generally ivy types can stand some shade everywhere and scented-leaf types, if grown mainly for foliage, will do well with semisun. Soil—garden types actually bloom better in a rather mediocre heavy soil and can stand considerable dryness. Ivy types like a more peaty soil. Avoid keeping constantly wet, particularly in winter, as root rot may develop. PROPAGATION: Hardy geraniums—seeds, sown in early spring and transplanted to the garden; division. Tender geraniums propagated mostly from cuttings (in fall for indoor winter bloom in the North or in spring for summer bloom). Can also be grown from seed; will bloom in about 4 to 6 months.

GLADIOLA (*Gladiolus*). Tender perennials grown from corms, generally planted for summer bloom in Northern gardens, lifted and stored dry in winter (although some may live through the winter if well mulched). There are some 200 species, with horticultural species now so modified that it is almost impossible to class them botanically. There are vast new forms, sizes and colors now available, most of them happily at reasonable prices (although not comparable to the mass supermarket and dime-store prices of the older, better-known types). Colors—white, cream, pinks, rose, yellow, gold, apricots, orange, lavenders, orchid, purple, crimson; bicolor types with contrasting throats; miniatures blotched, edged, feathered, and fringed; some even green (*dracocephalus*); and the new smoky varieties in dusty, dusky gray-rose, gray-violet; taupes with deep colored throats and markings. All-American glads, 1961, give some idea of the range. **Rusty**—deep smoky-red with petals blotched in bright red, edged in stark white. **China Blue**—with ruffled lavender-blue petals blotched parma-violet on lower petals. **Gypsy Dance**—ruffled petals of sharp scarlet-orange, splashed with yellow on lower petals. All, old and new alike, are marvelous as cut flowers—new flower buds opening daily in water with daily snipping of stems. CUL-

30. GLADIOLA (Orchid)

TURE: Sun; average soil. Plant corms for a succession of blooms every 2 weeks or so from May through June, even into early July. Average 4 inches deep for large bulbs, 3 inches for smaller bulbs (deeper in light soils). Stake tall growing ones (light bamboo is nice). Lift before ground freezes and store dry. PROPAGATION: Cormlets that form around old corm (bloom in 2 or 3 years). Seed is good for new varieties and strains; inexpensive but naturally takes longer to bloom.

GLORIOSA DOUBLE DAISY (Giant hybrid *Tetraploid Rudbeckia*). This plant is the result of what colchicine and genius did to the old Black-eyed Susan (*R. hirta*). This 1961 All-American Silver Medal Winner of Burpee has spectacular, round, golden balls like chrysanthemums. There are also semidoubles with brown-black velvety centers, to 4½ inches across on long, strong 3-foot stems; and singles to 5 inches across, in yellow to mahogany, some brilliantly bicolored. CULTURE: Sun,

31. GLORIOSA DOUBLE DAISY

average soil, bloom in midsummer and fall. Very robust, stand both extremes of heat and cold. Although perennial, they will bloom the first year if seed is sown early in spring. PROPAGATION: Division; seeds (not with hybrids).

GLOXINIA (*Sinningia speciosa*). If you live in a climate that is warm and muggy and have a shady sheltered spot and a sizable measure of pioneer spirit, by all means try growing these superb flowers. They grow beautifully in pots too, indoors or outdoors. Enormous velvety trumpet- or bell-shaped blossoms (half the size of the length of stems) with large textural leaves, some veined in white. The blooms

32. GLOXINIA

are spectacular both in colors and markings; pale violet-blue to deep purple-blue, blue with white borders, bright red, scarlet with white borders, deep rich scarlet, glistening pure white, pink—speckled, fringed, and ruffled. Tender tuberous perennials from Brazil, they like a temperature of not under 70 degrees and plenty of atmospheric humidity. CULTURE: Protect from hot sun and wind; light to rather deep shade suits them best. They need some good light or sun part of the day. Keep moist but be careful not to wet foliage in sun. After blooming, tubers should be dried off and stored cool (45 degrees ideal). Start tubers in January or February (peaty mixture in pots or "humusy" soil outdoors); place rounded part down and just barely cover with soil. As plantlets sprout, remove all but one if you want really showy specimens. Bloom in about 2 months. PROPAGATION: Division of tubers; leaf cuttings.

GUERNSEY LILY; RED SPIDER LILY (*Lycoris radiata*). Bulbous perennial, hardy to Md. and Tenn.; can sometimes be wintered over as far north as N.Y. with winter protection. Very showy, round clusters of red, orange, or white flowers (crested and curled) that appear before foliage. Increase very freely, soon filling garden with extravagant blooms. Late summer bloomers. CULTURE: Sun or shade; average soil, plant 4 to 6 inches apart, 2 inches deep. PROPAGATION: Offsets.

33. GUERNSEY LILY

HARDY AMARYLLIS; HALLII AMARYLLIS; CLUSTER AMARYLLIS; MAGIC LILY (*Lycoris squamigera: see Amaryllis under Perennials*). Pink, rose-lilac, fragrant, and unexpected because it suddenly makes its appearance in August on tall 2- to 3-foot stalks when the leaves produced in spring are dead and gone. Very unusual and showy, completely winter hardy—just do not forget you planted it

34. HARDY AMARYLLIS

and hoe it out during spring planting; robust grower. CULTURE: Sun or partial shade; any good soil. Grown from bulbs. Plant in September, 4 to 6 inches apart, 4 to 6 inches deep. PROPAGATION: Offsets.

HOLLYHOCK (*Althea rosea*). Tall stately plants whose lineage goes back hundreds of years in China and Europe. Most familiar to us as large, wide, open saucer-shaped flowers on 5- to 9-foot spikes. There are also doubles (like **Powderpuff,** shown here, or **Burpees Fancy Blend**) waved and fringed and frilled; and giants carnation-flowered, 4 to 5 inches across in lovely shades of pink, rose, scarlet, pale and deep yellows, salmon, white, red, maroon. Mostly biennials and semiperennials, although many persist for years and self-sow freely. There is also an annual (*see under Annuals*) which blooms during the first year if seed is started in February. Very floriferous, long blooming period from June until late summer. CULTURE: Very easy to grow, sun, even part shade. Requires little attention,

35. HOLLYHOCK (Burpee's Fancy Blend)

susceptible to rust however; pick diseased leaves promptly and destroy. PROPAGATION: Easy from seed usually planted in July for next year's bloom.

HORNED VIOLET; TUFTED PANSY (*Viola cornuta hybrida*). Impish little flowers on short stems in bright clear colors of apricot, purple, blue, yellow, white, produced among glistening dark-green foliage. Plants grow in lightly mounded clumps or spreading carpets. Good for rock gardens or when ground cover of clear color desired. Generally more reliable than pansies (*see under Perennials*). CULTURE: Sun, but will tolerate light shade; rich "humusy" soil. Apt to be short lived unless dead blossoms are promptly picked. Although hardy perennials, often behave as biennials, especially in regions having very hot summers. They like relatively cool, decidedly moist conditions. Mulching during hot weather

36. HORNED VIOLET

will greatly extend blooming. PROPAGATION: Seed (July and August); division; sometimes runners.

HYACINTH (*Hyacinthus orientales*). Far and away the most fragrant of the hardy spring bulbs, if not the most enduring; neither blooms nor bulbs last very long but the flower is entirely rewarding while they do. Very colorful range in white, pink, rose, red, yellow, blue, and purple. **Dutch Hyacinths** have the compact, funnel-shaped flowers thickly arranged on stiff erect spike. **Roman Hyacinth** is more slender, more graceful, with fewer, farther apart flowers. CULTURE: Sun; plant bulbs October 1 to 15, 3 to 6 inches deep, 4 to 6 inches apart in well-drained soil. Hyacinths tend to run out over the years and have to be replaced; allow foliage to yellow and die down naturally before cutting. In very cold climates a winter mulch will help bring them through. PROPAGATION: Division (not too successful).

37. HYACINTH

IRIS (*Iris*). For form, color, character, floriferousness, and ease of culture, Iris are hard to beat. There are many species and so many new hues constantly developed that Iris can now be had in almost any color or combinations of color, often pleasantly fragrant, blooming from spring into summer—sometimes again in the fall. They are roughly divided into three groups:

Bearded Iris—often called **German Iris** with characteristic beard on lower petals, swordlike, gray-green leaves, fleshy rhizomes usually pushing their way to the sur-

38. DWARF BEARDED IRIS (Moon Gleam)

face of the ground. These in turn break down into three heights: dwarf, intermediates, tall.

Dwarf Bearded Iris: Height 4 to 10 inches. Bloom April through early May. Enchanting, well-shaped flowers of superb color—all shades of yellow, blue, lilac, purple, cream, cherry red, maroon, mahogany, smoky tone; sometimes edged in white or brown with contrasting beards. Typical are **Guppy,** 6 inches, clear campanula blue; **Elf Charm,** 10 inches, cream, suffused blue; **Wee Turque,** 4 inches, multicolored turquoise-deep lavender. **Moon Gleam,** shown here, is a pure, clear light yellow with gold-dust beard, 5 to 6 inches. There are early, midseason, and late varieties, all excellent wherever a low-growing mass of color is wanted.

Intermediate Bearded Iris: As the name suggests, these are between dwarf and tall in size (2 feet), begin blooming just about when the dwarfs are finished and before the tall begin. Some also bloom in fall. They are similar in color to dwarf and tall, also having luminous yellows, ultramarine blue, coppery reds and white as **Zua** pictured here—icy-white, prettily frilled.

39. INTERMEDIATE BEARDED IRIS (Zua)

Tall Bearded Iris: Late May and June bloomers of excellent sculptural form, to 4 feet; self-colored, stippled, variegated, bicolored, in myriad tones and hues, from the most delicate tints to almost black. Newest is **Dame Fashion,** being perhaps the outstanding true pink—beginning life as a baby pink turning to a pure cotton-candy pink at maturity (4 feet). **Silver Rim,** shown here, is a sharp sapphire blue with frosted silvery borders; flowers of outstanding substance borne on 40-inch stems (new in 1961).

40. TALL BEARDED IRIS (Silver Rim)

Three Signals (shown here) is a satiny violet with unique white blaze on each fall; semiruffled, semiflaring, very large blooms; to

41. TALL BEARDED IRIS (Three Signals)

40 inches. CULTURE: Any good soil, well drained; plant shallowly, covering rhizomes with about 1 inch of soil. Do not worry when rhizomes push to top; they like to be sun baked. Full sun for good blooms; can take a little shade but with fewer blooms. Separate and replant every 2 to 3 years. Best time is right after flowering. Cut foliage back in fall to 4 inches.

Beardless Iris—Japanese, Siberian, Orientals characterized by graceful, slender green leaves, narrow rhizomes.

Japanese: Bloom after tall bearded—into July. Exquisite flowers, unique for their open, flattened look with graceful arching fall of petals, some measuring nearly a foot across. Single, double, and triple varieties in truly spectacular colors including pure white, reds, pinks, soft sky-blue, wisteria, dark blue, purples. **Pink Frost** shown here

42. JAPANESE IRIS (Pink Frost)

is a Marhigo: pale pale pink, all delicately ruffled, with double 8-inch flowers, 3½ feet. **Vain Victor** is an 8-inch double flat flowered, superbly patterned dark red-

43. JAPANESE IRIS (Vain Victor)

purple, white and violet. Typically Marhigo; 42 inches tall. **Iso No Kamone**—typifies the superb Higo strain, developed from *Iris Kaempferi,* with huge flowers up to a foot across, rich substance and velvety texture. This one is pure white, double, exquisitely ruffled; to 3½ feet. CULTURE: Responds well to rich organic soil; plenty of moisture while growing; well-adapted to wet ground beside stream, lake, or brook. Full sun for good blooms; can stand a little shade. Plant rhizomes 2 inches deep. Divide only when clumps become too large (August or September).

Siberian: A mixed group with many hybrids, both low- and tall-growing, having

44. SIBERIAN IRIS (Eric the Red)

graceful, slender grasslike leaves, slender rhizomes. Bloom in June with late, tall bearded varieties. Generally have smaller flowers, some with a clean, sculptured, almost architectural quality; mostly in shades of blue to purple, white, golds. Reds now being developed as **Eric, the Red,** shown here. **Gold Spot** is a chrysographes hybrid —mostly blue, purple, yellow; of trim but graceful habit, 12 to 16 inches. **White Heron** is part of the Spuria group (grown like Siberian but reaching heights of 6 feet)—a superb clean-cut blossom in white with suffused gold falls; to 48 inches. Spuria are generally more delicate to grow, come in a wider range of colors, some very fragrant. They are, however, easily grown from seed and, if you have rich soil, just might happen to do well. CULTURE: Sun; any good soil; plenty of moisture during the growing season or poor quality blooms. Plant 2 inches deep. Do not need dividing until 3 to 5 years; actually look better in good-sized clumps. Divide in spring or fall.

Bulbous Iris—Dutch, English, Spanish hybrids—Reputedly more difficult to grow,

45. DUTCH IRIS

these are unsurpassed as cut flowers (as those forced in florist shops amply testify). Similar to a large, crisp orchid, they come in superb colors—blues, yellows, golds, violets, bronze, lavenders, wine-purple, purple, white (English mainly in the orchid to purple range). Those who do succeed with them advise a rich, sandy loam with sharp drainage—nonacid for Dutch, on the acid side for English; full sun and an open exposure. Since they go dormant in June or early July, it is best to dig them up and store dry unless you can provide a well-drained soil. Plant 4 inches deep. If you do not store dry, it is advisable to provide a winter mulch in cold regions. Incidentally, these are surprisingly inexpensive.

KAFIR LILY (*Clivia miniata*). Subtropical perennial—tall, stately, with magnificent clusters of tubular scarlet flowers with

46. KAFIR LILY

yellow centers, dark-green, straplike, evergreen foliage. Cannot stand frost and must be grown in pots sunk in the garden during the summer in the North (excellent pot plant for indoors in winter). CULTURE: Good light, but protect from hot sun. Rich moist soil. POT CULTURE: Decrease water slightly after blooming but do not allow to get completely dry; new growth starts around Christmas; plants can stay in the same pot 3 to 4 years. PROPAGATION: Division (but hates it!); offsets.

LENTEN ROSE (*Helleborus orientalis*). Prized for its early blooming habit, its sturdiness, winter hardiness, and beautiful flowers, with the **Millet Hybrids** measuring to 3 inches across in colors of rose, raspberry,

47. LENTEN ROSE

maroon, pure white, speckled in reddish purple. Grows to 18 inches. May bloom as early as January in warm climates; February to April in the North. An even earlier bloomer is the **Christmas Rose** (*H. niger*) with flowering season from November to January (as you might expect). It has white flowers with shiny evergreen leaves. CULTURE: Partial shade, rich moist soil. PROPAGATION: Root division (late summer or fall); can remain undisturbed for years.

LILIES (*Lilium: see Day Lily, Calla Lily*). These are the true lilies grown from scaly bulbs, the most spectacular of all lilies, with today's hybrids available in all colors except blue, many exceptionally fragrant. Those shown here are but a very small sampling of the many superb species, varieties, and hybrids now offered. Unusually robust, all winter hardy.

Regal Lily (*L. regale*), shown here, has clusters of large (6 inches long) white trumpets touched with canary-yellow throat; shadings of lilac pink or purple on outside. Tall stalks to 5 feet. Highly perfumed. Blooms in July.

48. REGAL LILY

Goldband Lily (*L. auratum platyphyllum*), shown here. The colossus of all lilies, this particular specimen measuring 10 feet in height and producing over 80 flowers. Yours will probably reach 7 to 9 feet with anywhere from 15 to 30 blooms per stalk. The flowers are about 10 inches across with wide petals of clear crisp white, centered with a pale golden stripe, dotted with coral pink. Likes long, moist, cool growing season, August to September.

49. GOLDBAND LILY

Coral Lily (*L. tenuifolium* [*pumilum*]), shown here, has extremely graceful small nodding blooms 2 inches across with many recurved petals in glossy, waxy coral-scarlet, sometimes spotted. Variety *cernuum* is pale pink.

50. CORAL LILY

Aurelian Hybrids (*L. Sargentiae-Henryi Hybrids*) are tall, robust, with clusters of large open trumpets in colors ranging from white (**Snow Falcon,** shown here), cream, through apricots to near orange. Often cream suffused apricot. Newest is **Golden**

51. AURELIAN HYBRID LILY (Snow Falcon)

Splendor, pure, deep, uniform golden yellow, 5 to 7 feet tall, blooms in July.

Tiger Lily (*L. tigrinum*), shown here, is an old well-known favorite; single or double to 4 feet or more tall; large bright orange-red blooms, heavily spotted blue-black. Blooms August to September. CULTURE: All bulbs should be planted in the fall at different depth depending on species. Individual instructions usually sent with the shipment. In general, sun; a little light shade. Well-drained moist soil on the rich side. (Water settles among scales with ensuing rot.) Some bulbs root from the bottom, others (usually larger bulbs) also root at the base of the stem. These need 5 to 6 inches of soil above the bulbs. Small bulbs need no more than 2 to 3 inches of soil; large bulbs should be planted about twice their length. Seed is satisfactory for some, but apt to take several years. The **Regal Lily** is an exception, will produce blooms in 9 to 15 months. PROPAGATION: Separation of scales only worthy method with hybrids (2 to 3 years); seed; bulbils from axils of leaves; division.

52. TIGER LILY

LILY OF THE NILE; AFRICAN LILY (*Agapanthus africanus*). Summer-blooming tender perennial with tuberous rootstock, easily grown outdoors in frost-free regions, thrives in Florida or similar climates. Grown indoors in North in winter; outdoors in summer. Enormous umbels of fragrant dark-blue flowers on 3-foot stalks. Variety *Mooreanus* is smaller (to 18 inches) and hardier, with smaller blue flowers. *Albidus* has white flowers; variety *nana* is small

53. LILY OF THE NILE

and compact. Foliage is sometimes striped (*variegatus*). CULTURE: Sun or part shade and moist soil at all seasons. Plant tubers just below surface of soil (in pots, place growing end just level with surface of soil in 6-inch pot for dwarf varieties; double that or plant in large tub for tall varieties). PROPAGATION: Division of tubers; seed (takes 1 to 2 years for blooms).

LUPINE (*Lupinus*). Great garden favorites in England where humidity seems eminently suited to their culture. The tallest,

54. RUSSELL'S LUPINE

most stately of the perennials are shown here: **Russell's hybrids** (*L. polyphyllus hybrids*) with 3-foot spikes packed with flowers in extraordinary colors—yellow, orange, red, purple, white, pink, blue, and bicolors. Bloom 4 months from sowing. There are some good annuals, too, plus a **Tree Lupine** which is an 8-foot shrub, extensively grown in California, with yellow or white flowers often trained on trellises or up walls. CULTURE: Sun, well-drained but moist soil on the rich side. PROPAGATION: Easy from seed (likes cool weather germination). Difficult (but possible) to divide because of deep tap root.

LYTHRUM; PURPLE LOOSESTRIFE; WILLOW-HERB (*Lythrum Salicaria*). Wandlike 3-foot spikes of salmon pink (*roseum superbum*), deep rose-purple (*atropurpureum*), or white flowers (*tomentosum*) borne in late summer. Good for moist situations, winter-hardy in the North. CULTURE: Full sun, fairly heavy, moist soil ideal but will succeed also in light shade and lighter soil. Best to leave undisturbed

55. LYTHRUM

once established. PROPAGATION: Seed; division; cutting and rooting young shoots from base is best with named varieties.

MICHAELMAS DAISIES; HARDY ASTERS (*Aster*). (Not to be confused with the annual **China Aster** [*Callistephus*].) Compact, bushy, daisylike flowers up to 2½ inches across with single to triple rows of petals surrounding a bright yellow center. There are many named varieties of many species—dwarf to medium to tall growers in masses of both delicate and pungent colors: white, blues, lavenders, purples, pink, rose mauve violet. **Serenade,** shown here, is part of the 1961 collection of the

56. MICHAELMAS DAISY (Serenade)

new dwarf **Oregon Pacific** (late summer, fall-blooming) group; has large, delicate bluish-mauve flowers almost completely covering foliage (15 to 18 inches high). **Monarch** is a new strain; medium tall grower 2½ feet with flowers 2½ inches across in white, pale pinks, blues, lavender, red, purple. Mostly very hardy, very floriferous with long blooming season. Growing different varieties can give blooms from May until late fall. May to June: **Rock Aster** (*A. alpinus*) dwarf to 10 inches; blue, lilac, lavender, rose, white, purple, 1½-inch flowers. May to June: *A. Canbyi* to 2 feet; rose, red, purple, pink, white clusters. Also *A. subcaeruleus*, to 1 foot; solitary heads (2 to 3 inches) in pale lilac, blue (of uncertain hardiness in the North). Also *A. alpellus* hybrids, mauvy-blue range. June to July: *A. displostephioides*, to 2 feet; solitary large 3-inch flowers, blue-lavender range; not hardy in the North. Also *A. tibeticus*, 1 foot; bright blue heads to 2 inches across, very hardy and drought resistant. July to August: **Italian Aster** (*A. Amellus*), to 2 feet; violet-blue, purple, 1½-inch flowers in clusters. July to September: *A. Frikartii* hybrids; 2 feet; violet blue solitary heads to 3 inches across (beautiful but more difficult—cannot stand wet feet). June to September: *A. dumosus* hybrids, dwarf 6 to 8 inches, hardy to Massachusetts. September to October: *A. novi-belgii*, New York aster to 3 feet; bright blue-violet range. Also *A. novi-angliae*, New England aster to 5 feet; blue, pink, rose, violet, red, flowers to 2 inches across. CULTURE: Any well-drained soil in sun or partial shade. Thrives in all but desert regions (southern California and some southern sections); almost all winter hardy (exceptions noted); generally drought resistant. PROPAGATION: Division, preferably each spring; plant strong shoots from outside of clumps. Also in fall (plants shipped spring or fall). Seed (hybrids do not come true).

MILFOIL; YARROW (*Achillea Millefolium*). Dainty pompons of chrysanthemumlike flowers in large, heavily flowered

57. MILFOIL

clusters. Usually noted for its ability to bloom even under the most adverse conditions—poor soil and drought, although I would not recommend it. Hardy; grows 2 to 3 feet. Flowers usually white. Variety *rosea* has pink flowers; *Kelwayi*, magenta-red; *rubra*, dark pink. CULTURE: Sun, any average soil, set plants in spring, about 10 inches apart. For bloom from spring through late summer to early fall, cut back flowering stalks after blooms have faded. PROPAGATION: Division (every 3 or 4 years); cuttings; seeds.

MILK-AND-WINE LILY; CRINUM LILY (*Crinum campanulatum*). Part of the large handsome group of Crinum lilies of the Amaryllis family. Grown from some of

58. MILK-AND-WINE LILY

the largest bulbs in existence, some 20 inches or more in circumference. Funnel-shaped, lilylike flowers mostly in rosy red, pink, white with colored streaking; to 3 or 4 feet. Of simple culture, very persistent in the South, forming large showy clumps during spring and summer. Not hardy, should be taken up during the winter in northern climates and stored dry. The following three species, however, are hardy as far as New York in protected locations: *Powellii*—red and its variety *albume* (pure white), waxen, trumpet-lily-shaped; *Moorei*—large, flaring, bell-shaped, white-flushed red; *longifolium*—long fragrant flower trumpets in pink and white. CULTURE: Light sun; semishade; average good soil. Consult dealer for planting depth of bulbs—differs with species, variety, and locality. Do not disturb unless imperative; replanting often sets plant back several years. PROPAGATION: Offsets; seed (blooms in 3 to 5 years).

ORIENTAL POPPY (*Papaver orientale*). Superb while they last (about 2 to 3 weeks) with large clumps of flamboyant flowers, but a rather unsightly mess when they go dormant in August, so be prepared! Bloom in early summer. Although originally available only in a flaming orangy red, contemporary forms include lovely soft shades of pink, white, rose, lavender, salmon-orange, fire-red, maroon, and deep mahogany. Deep silken saucers (some double) up to 10 inches across. Robust growers up to 4 feet. Reliably hardy in cold regions; also do well in mild-wintered regions (but not where summers are excessively dry and winters constantly warm). CULTURE: Full sun. Plant root at end of dormant season

59. ORIENTAL POPPY

(late August or early September) about 2 to 3 inches deep (a full grown clump takes about 3 feet of space). Plant just deep enough to permit leaves to show. Water well. PROPAGATION: Division, every 3 to 4 years. Use a sharp knife and divide fleshy root, allowing a section of crown for each piece. Also from root cutting. Cut into 3-inch pieces and set vertically in ground with top of cutting nearest surface of ground. Seed (do not come true).

ORNAMENTAL ONION (*Allium*). Some of the prettier members of the onion family and just as easy to grow from bulbs. Winter hardy, generally robust, often used for naturalizing or rockeries. *A. karataviense*, shown here; 3-inch ball of very pretty star-

60. ORNAMENTAL ONION

like, white-with-purple flowers; cupped in wide orchid leaves, grows to 10 inches. *A. giganteum* grows to a stately 4 feet with large floriferous 4-inch ball of bright lilac blooms. CULTURE: Sun or semishade, average soil. PROPAGATION: Division.

PAINTED DAISY; PERSIAN DAISY; PYRETHRUM (*Chrysanthemum coccineum; Pyrethrum hybridum var.*). These big beautiful double Pyrethrum look more and more like a chrysanthemum—the genus to which they belong. Colors—white, rose, flesh-pink, pink, crimson, and red. Better known are the single daisylike types, often 3 inches across in white, pink, lilac, rose, red, borne on tall stalks 2 to 4 feet in height with dainty fernlike deep-green foliage. Very easy to grow, robust, winter hardy. Unfortunately they bloom but a short period in May to June, but if you cut flowers be-

61. PAINTED DAISY (Double)

fore they go to seed, plant may produce another stalk. CULTURE: Full sun, average well-drained soil. PROPAGATION: Divide every 2 to 3 years in spring; also easy from seed but seeds of named varieties do not come true.

PANSY (*Viola tricolor*). Colorful, romantic little flowers with a tradition dating back to the seventeenth century—the name itself

62. PANSY

coming from the French word *pensée* meaning thought and remembrance. Irresistible in early spring when boxes of them in full bloom are available at every supermarket and roadside nursery but not too easy to keep from becoming straggly and to carry over to the following year. Although perennials, they behave more like biennials or even annuals, generally going into a decline when hot weather sets in. Low-growing chunky plants, ideal for rock gardens and nooks and crannies. Flowers: modern strains to 3 inches across in just about any color and combinations of color namable—some ruffled and curled. White, pale blue, yellow, lavender, purple, chocolate, near pinks, and terra cotta, all delicately fragrant. CULTURE: Sun; moist, humusy soil. Do not crowd them—plant about 7 or 8 inches apart. Mulch to keep them cool and blooming. Pluck all dead blossoms promptly but do not overpick live flowers as plants may well be encouraged to bloom themselves to death. Cut back straggly stalks to 2 or 3 inches and keep new shoots coming along. Mulch lightly over winter in very cold regions. With luck they may reappear the following spring. PROPAGATION: Seed from July to the middle of August; division.

PATIENCE PLANT; PATIENT LUCY (*Impatiens*). Tender perennial grown as summer bedding plant in cold regions, practically the mainstay of my dining-room terrace, it being one of the few plants I know to bloom freely and continuously with but a few spotty hours of sun daily. Most species in cultivation are usually *I. Sultanii, I. Holstii, I. Oliveri, platypetala,* with hybrids not too clearly defined. **Scarlet Baby,** shown here, is extra dwarf to 6

63. PATIENCE PLANT (Scarlet Baby)

inches (height generally varies from 1 to 3 feet) in clear scarlet. Other colors in soft shades of pink, rose, salmon, coral, white. New in 1960 was **American Beauty,** the first true, clear bright red of that famous name. Size of flowers generally 1 to 1¾ inches across. CULTURE: Semisun or light shade (should have some sun sometime during the day). Moist (but not constantly sopping) peaty soil. PROPAGATION: Easy from seed, blooming 3 months after sown, and once you have one plant, you have a dozen. Cuttings root readily in water (in a matter of days during growing season), giving you more plants than you can use. I generally take cuttings in fall to bring indoors, root them in water, pot them for the winter; take cuttings from potted plants again in early spring and have dozens of healthy plants ready to bloom by the time the weather is warm enough to set outdoors. And the more cuttings you take, the bigger and bushier and more floriferous the mother plant!

PEONY (*Paeonia*). Hardy sturdy perennials —great garden favorites as far back as flower records have been kept. Very long lasting, often handed down from generation to generation with many named varieties still as popular today as they were 100 years ago. Numerous modern forms of larger, longer lasting blooms extend blooming season several weeks (May and June). Grow 2 to 3½ feet tall in shrublike manner with highly decorative deep green leaves. Flowers: large, mostly from white, cream, pinks to reds, to purple, some yellows tipped with red, some pure yellows, some bicolored, many delicately fragrant. Singles are like a large wild rose. Doubles are flattened, rose-shaped, ball-like. Japanese types have single petals with frilled or shredded stamens, shown here. Anemone types are like the Japanese with broadened incurving stamens. CULTURE: Sun preferred but very light shade tolerated, rich clayey soil but well-drained and plenty of water during growing period. After blooming they can stand considerable drought but bloom better the following year if kept watered. Plant tubers 2 inches deep about 3 feet apart in early fall (September through October); also possible in spring. Heavy feeders; fertilize annually, just as buds begin to appear. When cutting flowers, be sure to

64. JAPANESE PEONY

leave at least 3 or 4 leaves on each stalk to manufacture food for next year's blooms. Stake if necessary. Not always successful in the South, since they require a period of cold during dormancy, but once established plants often come through admirably. PROPAGATION: Division (leave about 5 growth buds or eyes); seed (but hybrids will not come true).

PERIWINKLE (*Vinca rosea*). This periwinkle is a tender perennial, sometimes called **Madagascar Periwinkle** (*see Periwinkle, Creeping Madagascar Periwinkle in Trailers, Ground Covers, Creepers*). Grows

65. PERIWINKLE

well outdoors in warm climates; grown up North as an annual. Pretty bushy compact plant (12 inches) covered with waxy phloxlike blooms (1½ inches across) in rosy pinks to rosy purples, crimson, white. Sturdy, everblooming. CULTURE: Not fussy, prefers rich sandy soil and sun, but will grow in dry or wet conditions and some shade. I have even seen it growing in bone-dry coral sands in Florida. PROPAGATION: Seeds (start them early indoors in North); cuttings.

PINKS (*Dianthus: see Pinks under Annuals, Carnations, Sweet William under Perennials and Biennials*). A widely hybridized, confused family of deliciously fragrant, brilliantly flowered perennials. Usually listed as **Garden Pinks** and variously descended from

66. GARDEN PINK

3 species: **Cottage** or **Grass Pink** (*D. plumarius*), **Clove Pink** (*D. caryophyllus*), and **Cluster Pink** (*D. latifolius*—itself a hybrid). Flowers: single or double in a profusion of colors, white, pink, crimson, red, mauve, purple, yellow, with fringed or toothed petals often ringed with contrasting color; pretty grasslike, bluish semievergreen foliage. Many alpine dwarf varieties usually recommended for rock gardens. Height from 10 inches to 2 feet depending on the variety, with *D. plumarius,* shown here, averaging 18 inches. CULTURE: Full sun, well-drained soil with plenty of water. Will not tolerate poor, sunbaked soil. Do best where summers are cool and moist, winters relatively mild. Rigorous shearing of foliage will keep them neat and flowering. **Cottage** or **Grass Pinks** hardiest throughout United States. Varieties of *D. latifolius* generally require protection in the North; and **Clove Pinks** should be protected north of New York. PROPAGATION: Division simplest; cuttings; layering; seeds are always a happy surprise. Plants seed themselves freely, but do not come true to type.

RANUNCULUS (*Ranunculus*). These Tecolote giants of the buttercup family are semidouble or double with camellialike blooms 3 inches or more across on strong stems to 15 inches high. Clear brilliant

67. RANUNCULUS

colors in a wonderful range, straw, gold, scarlet, pink, many variegated, ringed or tipped with deeper color. Plant in North for spring and summer bloom; take up and store dry over winter. Not reliable north of Washington, D.C., but winter protection may carry them over. CULTURE: Full sun, average soil. PROPAGATION: Division of tuberous root.

SAGE (*Salvia*). How will you have it? As a hardy perennial in the culinary garden for seasoning (*S. officinalis*) or as a semihardy, perennial, ornamental flowering plant with white woolly leaves? Here are some of the species available to you. Treat as an annual in the North. **Blue** or **Mealycup Sage** (S. *farinacea*), shown here, grows to 3 feet, has

68. BLUE SAGE

rich, 1½-inch, Wedgwood-blue, airy flowers with white to violet calyxes in whorled racemes to 8 inches long. Also in white. **Gentian Sage** (S. *patens*) to 2½ feet, has large, clear, 2-inch-long, intense indigo-blue flowers, broad, tubular, and lipped. **Great Azure Sage** (S. *Pitcheri*) to 4 feet with dense clear blue to white, 1-inch flowers. **Violet Sage** (usually S. *superba* or S. *sylvestris*, wrongly known as S. *nemorosa*) is a hardy perennial to 3 feet, slender racemes of purple-violet or white flowers, some with red bracts. **Scarlet Sage** (S. *splendens*) is the tallest and largest flowered, with graceful sprays of trenchant scarlet blooms to 3 feet tall. Many other scarlet varieties are also listed from dwarf, intermediate to tall in various clear and strong scarlet reds. CULTURE: Sun or partial shade; any good soil. Very sturdy and drought resistant. Easy from seed; when treated as annuals, sow indoors in February or March to give them a head start for a long blooming period.

SCABIOSA (*Scabiosa*). Many species of perennials and annuals, the latter often called **Pincushion Flowers** (S. *atropurpurea*) because of their globular appearance. Perennial species have more flattened heads such as the House Giant hybrid **Blue Bonnet** (S. *caucasica* hybrid), shown here. It is a strong sturdy grower (to 3 feet) with giant, ruffled blooms on tall stems in colors from icy white to lavender, light blue, azure to ultramarine. Blooms June to September and makes an excellent cutting flower. S. *graminifolia* is an attractive dwarf with sky-blue flowers (to 12 inches) good for rock garden. CULTURE: Of the easiest; full sun, but thrives with little care.

69. SCABIOSA (Blue Bonnet)

Plant seeds either in the open in spring (or fall in mild climates); many bloom the first year. PROPAGATION: Frequent division beneficial.

SHASTA DAISY (*Chrysanthemum maximum* hybrids). So many different flowers go under the name of Shasta Daisies, from the simple white daisylike 2-inch flowers with yellow center, to the shredded, frilled, semidoubles, to the rich double-white form shown here with huge 6-inch chrysanthemumlike flowers on 2½-foot stems. All are easy to grow if frequently divided. In very wet soils they may behave like biennials. All are winter hardy. Bloom June, July, August. CULTURE: Full sun or partial sun; well-drained average soil. Set plants 1 foot apart. PROPAGATION: Divide every second year; seed (but do not allow to seed them-

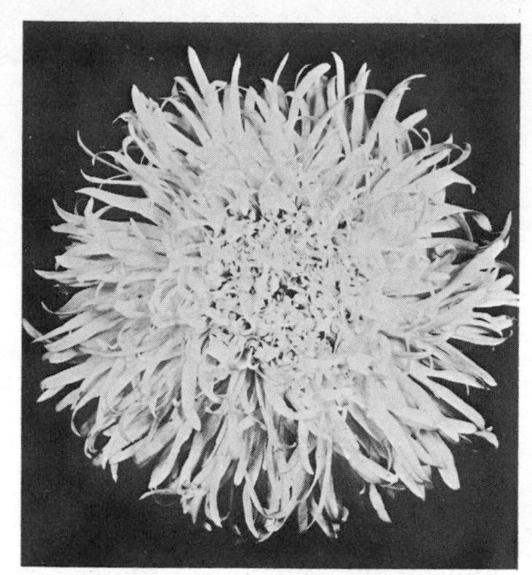

70. SHASTA DAISY

selves unless you like surprises—seeds will not come true).

SPIDER LILY; PERUVIAN DAFFODIL; BASKET FLOWER (*Hymenocalles calathina,* commonly sold as *Ismene calathina*). A favorite spring-into-summer flowering bulb with large, white, waxy blooms fringed and fragrant, borne 4 to 5 on each 2-foot scape; throat striped in green. Actually winter hardy, being a native of the

71. SPIDER LILY

Andes, but it does not seem to bloom if left in the ground except in the South where it persists easily year after year. In the North, it should be lifted and stored dry in late fall, allowing foliage to ripen until winter killed. Variety *sulphurea* is pale yellow. CULTURE: Bulbs started in April or May in the South bloom in about a month. In the North, plant about May 15, 4 to 6 to 8 inches deep (consult local dealer) in rich, peaty soil. PROPAGATION: Offsets.

STAR OF BETHLEHEM; CHINKERICHEE (*Ornithogalum thyrsoides*). Tender bulbs with dense spikes of 30 to 40 white

72. STAR OF BETHLEHEM

starry flowers clustered on triangular heads 18 inches tall. Hardy from North Carolina on south. When in doubt, take up and store over the winter. CULTURE: Sun, average soil. Plant bulbs 6 inches deep. Can sometimes be made to flower the same year from seed. PROPAGATION: Offsets.

SWEET WILLIAM (*Dianthus barbatus: also see Sweet William under Annuals; see Pinks and Carnations under Perennials and Biennials; see Pinks under Annuals*). One of the oldest known garden flowers with large showy clusters of phloxlike blossoms, single or double in many shades of pink, scarlet, crimson, watermelon, purple, copper, white, often varicolored, with eye and fringe of contrasting color. Delicately scented, of neat compact habit, generally 10 to 18 inches tall. Charming new dwarf varieties bloom at only 4 inches tall, making a low, dense, very floriferous carpet for rock gardens. Relatively hardy perennials, plants are usually treated as biennials; although if blossoms are snipped before they form seed and plants are kept moist, they may produce for years. There are also some annual types (see under

73. SWEET WILLIAM (Double)

Annuals) which will flower the first year. CULTURE: Full sun, any good average, well-drained soil. Very easy to start from seed outdoors in May or June and transplant in August for blooms the following year. May also be propagated by layering (sometimes preferable with double-flowered types as they do not always come true from seeds).

TIGER FLOWERS; LEOPARD FLOWERS; MEXICAN SHELL FLOWERS (*Tigridia Pavonia vars.*). Summer-blooming tender bulb which must be taken up in fall where winters are cold. Have been known to winter over as far north as North Carolina. Brilliant, exotic flowers in scarlet, salmon, red, rose, pale yellow, golden yellow, orange—blotched, streaked or spotted with red, purple, and brown; often tinged pink, lilac, and apricot. They grow to 2½ feet tall. CULTURE: Full sun in the North, part shade in the South. Plant bulbs 3 to 4 inches deep, 6 inches apart, in late spring for July to August bloom; lift before frost

74. TIGER FLOWER

and store in dry place over the winter. PROPAGATION: Offsets; seeds (but may not come true to type).

TRANSVAAL DAISY; GERBERA (*Gerberia Jamesonii* hybrids). Tender perennial with huge daisylike blooms (4 inches) on long graceful stems (1 to 2 feet). Superb colors, both brilliant and pale—amber, salmon, apricot, yellow, terra-cotta, orange,

75. TRANSVAAL DAISY

flame, flesh, pink, rose, ruby, scarlet. In cold regions may be grown outdoors in the summer, indoors in pots in the winter. CULTURE: Sun or very light shade; sandy peaty loam suits them best; sharp drainage is essential or crown rot apt to develop. Make planting hole deep, as roots like to go straight down; keep crown a little above ground level. PROPAGATION: Division (after several years, separate roots so each portion has two buds).

TUBEROUS BEGONIA (*Begonia tuber-hybrida*). These superb plants have become almost as popular in northern gardens as they are in mild climates, but they must be brought in in the fall since they are tender and can stand no frost at all. Enormous flowers (up to 8 inches across) in white, pink, rose, red, yellow; single or camellia- or carnation-shaped flowers, very full and frilled. CULTURE: Light shade or part sun; moist, rich peaty soil. Plant in sheltered location, tubers level with soil surface, hollow side up. In northern climates, start

76. TUBEROUS BEGONIA

tubers in peat and sand in early March. Transfer to garden after danger of frost is over. Dry and store during dormant period (plants die back in early fall; dry off slowly and store in dry peat or sand in cool dry place). PROPAGATION: Seeds (takes 2 years); division of tubers.

TULIPS (*Tulipa*). Hardy spring-blooming bulbs (May and June), of innumerable shapes and colors: single, double, bicolor, striped, spotted; cup-shaped, bell-shaped, lily-shaped, saucer-shaped, peonylike, feathered or fringed in every color but blue —even a real green. There are also dwarf, semidwarf, medium, and tall varieties of some 60 species and several thousand horticultural forms, commonly named **cottage, breeders, Darwins, parrot,** and the **botanical** or **specie tulips.** Dwarfs are especially

77. DARWIN TULIP

78. BOTANICAL TULIP

79. DWARF TULIP

suited to rock gardens. CULTURE: Full sun for good flowers, but some shade tolerated. Need well-drained soil or will rot. Plant anywhere from 3 to 6 inches deep, 4 to 6 to 8 inches apart (the deeper they are planted the later they will bloom). Usually planted in October in the North; in December in the South (after a cooling off period in the refrigerator of some 4 to 6 weeks). Allow leaves to die down naturally after flowering. Some hard workers prefer to dig them up (do not break leaves) and heel them in a shady place to ripen; then store in cool, dark, dry place. True, they do tend to deteriorate when left to themselves, but if you pick off dead blooms, they will probably last 3 years or so, at which time they should be lifted and divided anyhow.

TWELVE APOSTLES; APOSTLE PLANT (*Marica*). A beautiful tender perennial, so called because the attractive fanlike tufts usually consist of 12 sword-shaped leaves. The fragrant blooms look half iris, half orchid, and are borne on tall, stiff stalks. The **Fan Iris** (*M. northiana*) grows to 3 feet and has very fragrant flowers 4 inches across, pure white with violet marking. The smaller *M. gracilis*, shown here, grows to 1½ feet, has white flowers 2 inches across marked with yellow, brown, and blue. *M. caerulea* (to 2½ feet) has bright blue or lilac flowers 4 inches across, barred in yellow, white, and brown. Excellent pot plants for the North. Hardy only in mild regions—Florida and similar climates. May be planted out early in fall and although they make foliage, they will survive the winter. CULTURE: Sun or part shade; average soil with good drainage. PROPAGATION: Division.

80. TWELVE APOSTLES

More Perennials and Biennials

ACONITE; MONKSHOOD (*Aconitum Napellus*). To 4 feet, with dark-blue flowers in June, July. Hardy; part shade.

ADAMS NEEDLE (*Yucca filamentosa*). To 12 feet with whitish flowers in June, July. Hardy; sun.

ALPINE FORGET-ME-NOT (*Myosotis alpestris* [*sylvatica*]). To 8 inches with blue flowers in May, June. Protect in North; part shade.

AMETHYST ERYNGO (*Eryngium amethystinum*). To 1½ feet with blue flowers in June to September. Hardy; sun.

AMUR ADONIS (*Adonis amurensis*). To 1½ feet with yellow, pink to white flowers in March. Hardy; sun or part shade.

ASPIDISTRA (*Aspidistra elatior*). To 2½ feet with purple-brown flowers, winter blooming. Tender, sturdy, tolerates poor light, poor soil.

AUTUMN MONKSHOOD (*Aconitum autumnale*). To 5 feet with blue, mauve, white flowers from June to September. Hardy; part shade.

BABY'S BREATH (*Gypsophila paniculata*). To 3 feet with white flowers in July, August. Hardy; sun or light shade.

BASTARD SPEEDWELL (*Veronica spuria*). To 2 feet with blue flowers in May, June. Hardy; part shade.

BEARGRASS (*Xerophyllum tenax*). To 5 feet with white flowers in June, July. Protect in North; sun.

BEE-BALM; FRAGRANT BALM; OSWEGO TEA (*Monarda didyma*). To 2 to 3 feet with pink, red flowers in June to August. Hardy; part shade.

BIG BETONY; WOUNDWORT (*Stachys grandiflora*). To 3 feet with white, pink, mauve, violet, purple flowers in June, July. Hardy; sun.

BLACK COHOSH (*Cimicifuga racemosa*). To 8 feet with fragrant white flowers in July. Hardy; part shade.

BLACKBERRY LILY (*Belamcanda chinensis*). To 4 feet with orange flowers, spotted red in July, August. Blackberry-like seeds. Hardy; sun.

BLACKBUD INULA (*Inula Royleana*). To 2 feet with orange-yellow flowers in July, August. Hardy; sun.

BLANKET FLOWER (*Gaillardia aristata*). To 2 to 3 feet with crimson, yellow flowers July to November. Hardy; sun.

BLUE GENTIAN (*Gentiana sceptrum, G. Menziesii*). To 4 feet with clusters of dark-blue flowers dotted with green in June. Good for Pacific-coast climates; sun or light shade.

BLUE WILD INDIGO (*Baptisia australis*). To 6 feet with indigo-blue flowers in June, July. Protect in North; sun or part shade.

BLUEBELL; HAREBELL (*Campanula rotundifolia*). To 1½ feet with bright blue flowers from June to August. Hardy; sun or part shade.

BOUNCING BET (*Saponaria officinalis, Silene Saponaria*). To 3 feet with pink or white flowers May to September. Evening blooming. Hardy. Easy in sun or part shade; any soil.

BOWSTRING HEMP (*Sansevieria* varieties). From 1 to 5 feet with whitish or yellowish flowers in winter. Grown for foliage —often variegated and mottled. Tender; sun or shade.

BUSH LADYBELL (*Adenophora Potaninii*). To 3 feet with blue-violet flowers in July, August. Hardy; sun.

BUTTERFLY WEED; PLEURISY ROOT (*Asclepias tuberosa*). To 3 feet with orange flowers in July, August. Hardy; sun or light shade.

CAROLINA THERMOPSIS (*Thermopsis caroliniana*). To 5 feet with yellow flowers in June, July. Hardy; sun; dry soil.

CHILEAN ALSTROEMERIA (*Alstroemeria chilensis*). To 4 feet with orange- to red-fringed flowers in July, August. Tender bulb; in October plant 6 inches deep, 12 inches apart.

CHILOE AVENS (*Geum chiloense*). To 2 feet with scarlet, golden-yellow flowers in June to August. Hardy; sun or light shade.

CHIMNEY BELLFLOWER (*Campanula pyramidalis*). To 5 feet with pale blue, white flowers in July, August. Hardy; sun or light shade.

CHINESE LANTERN PLANT; WINTER CHERRY (*Physalis Alkekengi*). To 2 feet with white flowers July to October. Red fruit. Protect in North; sun. Often grown as an annual but needs long growing period.

CLETHRA LOOSESTRIFE (*Lysimachia clethroides*). To 3 feet with white flowers July to September. Hardy; sun or light shade; moist to boggy locations.

CLUMP SPEEDWELL (*Veronica maritima var. subsessilis*). To 2 feet with deep blue flowers July to September. Hardy; half shade.

COLUMBINE MEADOW RUE (*Thalictrum aquilegifolium*). To 3 feet with cream-white sepals, purple-pink stamens. Blooms May to July. Hardy; sun or light shade.

CROCUS TRITONIA (*Tritonia crocusmaeflora*). From 3 to 4 feet with orange-crimson flowers July to October. Hardy bulb; in May, plant 3 to 4 inches deep, 3 to 6 inches apart.

CROWN IMPERIAL (*Fritillaria imperialis*). From 2 to 4 feet with purplish, brick or yellow-red flowers April, May. Hardy bulb; in September, plant 6 inches deep, 6 inches apart.

CUSICK CAMAS (*Camassia Cusickii*). To 3 feet with blue flowers in May. Hardy bulb. In September, plant 3 to 6 inches deep, 4 inches apart.

DAME'S ROCKET; DAME'S VIOLET (*Hesperis matronalis*). To 3 feet with lilac, light purple to white flowers in May to July. Hardy; sun or light shade.

DELAVAY'S INCARVILLEA (*Incarvillea Delavayi*). To 2 feet. Rose-purple flowers with yellow tubes in June, July. Hardy; sun.

DESERT CANDLE (*Eremurus Elwesii*). To 2 feet with pink flowers in July. Semihardy, protect in North. Sun or light shade.

DESERT CANDLE (*Eremurus himalaicus*). To 3 feet with white flowers in racemes in July, August. Protect in North. Sun; light shade.

DUSTY MILLER; BEACH WORMWOOD (*Artemisia Stelleriana*). To 2½ feet with white woolly leaves, racemes of small yellow flowers in August. Hardy; sun.

ENGLISH WALLFLOWER (*Cheiranthus Cheiri*). To 2½ feet with yellow to yellow-brown flowers in May. Semihardy, protect in the North; sun or part shade.

FALL DAFFODIL; AMARYLLIS LUTEA (*Sternbergia lutea*). From 4 to 6 inches with yellow flowers in September, October. Hardy bulb; in August or September, plant 6 inches deep, 6 inches apart.

FERN ASPARAGUS (*Asparagus plumosus*). To 2½ feet with whitish flowers, purplish-black berries. Grown for its feathery foliage. Winter blooming. Tender; semishade.

FLAX (*Linum perenne*). To 2½ feet with azure-blue flowers May to September. Hardy; sun.

FLEABANE (*Erigeron macranthus*). To 2½ feet with lilac, bluish purple flowers in July, August. Hardy; sun.

FLORAL FIRE CRACKER (*Brevoortia Ida-Maia*). To 3 feet with scarlet flowers, tipped green May to July. Half-hardy bulb; in September, plant 2 inches deep, 4 inches apart. Protect in North.

FLOWERING SPURGE (*Euphorbia corollata*). To 3 feet with white flowers in July, August. Hardy; sun.

GAS PLANT; BURNING BUSH (*Dictamnus albus*). To 3 feet with white flowers in June, July. Hardy; sun.

GIBRALTAR CANDYTUFT (*Iberis gibraltarica*). To 1 foot with lilac, light purple flowers April to June. Evergreen foliage. Protect in North; part shade.

GLACIER LILY (*Erythronium grandiflorum*). To 2 feet with bright yellow flowers in April and May. Tender bulb; good for West Coast. From September to November, plant 3 inches deep, 3 inches apart.

GLOBE CENTAUREA (*Centaurea macrocephala*). To 3 feet with yellow flowers in July, August. Hardy; sun or light shade.

GLOBE FLOWER (*Trollius europaeus*). To 2 feet with yellow flowers May to August. Hardy; good for damp places. Sun or light shade.

GLORY OF THE SNOW (*Chinonodoxa Luciliae*). From 3 to 8 inches with blue flowers with white center. Blooms March to May. Hardy bulb. In September, plant 3 inches deep, 3 to 4 inches apart.

GOAT'S RUE (*Galega officinalis*). To 3 feet with purplish-blue flowers June to September. Hardy; sun.

GOATSBEARD (*Aruncus sylvester, Spiraea Aruncus*). To 7 feet with white flowers on upright spike in July. Hardy; sun.

GOLDEN FLAX (*Linum flavum*). To 2 feet with yellow flowers May to September. Hardy; sun or light shade.

GOLDEN GLOBE TULIP (*Calochortus amabilis*). To 1½ feet with yellow flowers in June. Tender bulb. In September, plant 3 inches deep, 3 inches apart.

GOLDEN MARGUERITE (*Anthemis tinctoria*). To 3 feet with yellow flowers May to October. Hardy; sun.

GREEN GYPSOPHILA (*Gypsophila acutifolia*). To 3 feet with white flowers in July, August. Hardy; sun; dry soil.

HELIOTROPE (*Heliotropium arborescens*). To 4 feet with vanilla-scented violet, purple, varying to white, flowers June to September. Tender; sun.

HIMALAYAN CINQUEFOIL (*Potentilla atrosanguinea*). To 1½ feet with red, purple flowers June to August. Hardy; part shade.

INDIAN-PHYSIC (*Gillenia trifoliata*). To 4 feet with white, pinkish flowers in June, July. Hardy; sun.

INDIAN REED (*Canna indica vars.*). From 3 to 6 feet with yellow and red flowers in July, August. Tender; sun. Lift and store roots over winter in North.

ITALIAN BUGLOSS (*Anchusa azurea*). To 5 feet with blue flowers June to August. Hardy; sun.

JACOB'S-LADDER (*Polemonium caeruleum*). To 3 feet with blue flowers April to June. Hardy; sun or light shade; moist soil.

JACOB'S-ROD (*Asphodeline lutea*). To 4 feet with yellow flowers in June, July. Hardy; sun.

JAPANESE ANEMONE (*Anemone japonica*). To 3 feet with purplish, red, rose, white yellow-centered flowers September to frost. Protect in North; shade.

LEOPARD'S BANE (*Doronicum caucasicum*). To 2 feet with daisylike flowers in May, June. Hardy; sturdy; sun or light shade.

MALTESE CROSS (*Lychnis chalcedonica*). To 3 feet with scarlet flowers in June, July. Hardy; sun.

MATILIJA POPPY (*Romneya Coulteri*). From 4 to 8 feet with white flowers June to October. Tender to semihardy, might survive a sheltered location as far as New York. Sun or light shade.

MIST FLOWER (*Eupatorium coelestinum*). To 3 feet with blue to violet flowers in August, September. Hardy; sun.

MOUNTAIN ARNICA (*Arnica montana*). To 2 feet with heads of yellow flowers in July, August. Hardy; sun or light shade.

MOUNTAIN BLUET (*Centaurea montana*). To 2 feet with blue flowers May to September. Hardy; sun.

MULLEIN PINK (*Lychnis Coronaria*). To 3 feet with crimson flowers in June, July. Hardy; half shade.

OLYMPIC MULLEIN (*Verbascum olympicum*). To 5 feet with yellow flowers in July. Hardy; sun.

PEARL EVERLASTING (*Anaphalis margaritacea*). To 3 feet with white flowers in July, August. Hardy; sun.

PHLOX (*Phlox maculata*). To 3 feet with pink, purple flowers in June, July. Hardy; sun.

PHLOX, EARLY PERENNIAL (*Phlox suffruticosa*). To 3 feet with purple varieties to rose, white flowers in June, July. Hardy; sun.

PHLOX, SUMMER PERENNIAL (*Phlox paniculata var.*). To 4 feet with various colored flowers June to September. Hardy; sun.

PINK TURTLEHEAD (*Chelone Lyonii*). To 3 feet with rose-purple flowers in August, September. Hardy; part shade; moist soil to swampy places.

PITCHER HELIOPSIS (*Heliopsis helianthoides var. Pitcheriana*). To 3 feet with yellow flowers June to October. Hardy; sun.

PLANTAIN-LEAVED LEOPARD'S BANE (*Doronicum plantagineum*). To 5 feet with yellow daisylike flowers in May, June. Hardy; sun.

PLUME POPPY (*Macleaya cordata*). To 8 feet with panicles of cream flowers, large (8 inches across) green leaves, white beneath, in July, August. Hardy; sun.

POPPY-FLOWERED ANEMONE (*Anemone coronaria*). To 1½ feet with shades and combinations of red, white, and blue, in early spring to June. Hardy; part shade.

PURPLE CONEFLOWER (*Echinacea purpurea*). To 4 feet with purple to white flowers July to October. Hardy; sun or light shade.

QUEEN OF THE MEADOW (*Filipendula Ulmaria*). To 6 feet with white flowers in June, July. Hardy; sun or light shade; best in moist soil.

QUEEN OF THE PRAIRIE (*Filipendula rubra*). To 8 feet with peach-pink flowers in June, July. Hardy; sun or light shade; best in moist soil.

RED VALERIAN (*Centranthus ruber*). To 3 feet with crimson, pale red flowers in June, July. Hardy; sun or part shade.

ROSE MALLOW (*Hibiscus Moscheutos*). To 8 feet with pink, rose flowers in August, September. Protect in North; shade. Moist soil to swampy locations.

ROVER BELLFLOWER; FALSE RAMPION (*Campanula rapunculoides*). To 3 feet with blue, violet, purple flowers in July, August. Hardy; sun or part shade.

ST. BERNARD LILY (*Anthericum Liliago*). To 3 feet with white flowers in July, August. Semihardy bulb. In May, plant 4 inches deep, 6 inches apart. Protect in North.

ST. JOHNS WORT (*Hypericum Ascyron*). To 2 feet with yellow flowers August to October. Tender; shade.

SEA-LAVENDER, BIGLEAF (*Limonium latifolium*). To 2 feet with calyx white, corolla blue in June, July. Hardy; sun or light shade.

SEA-LAVENDER, NOTCHLEAF (*Limonium sinuatum*). To 2 feet with calyx blue, corolla yellowish, white in June, July. Sun or light shade; grown as annual.

SILVER KING ARTEMESIA (*Artemisia albula*). To 3½ feet; foliage: white, feathery aromatic sprays; shoots may be cut and dried for winter bouquet. Hardy; sun.

SMALL GLOBE THISTLE (*Echinops Ritro*). To 2 feet with blue, white flowers July to September. Hardy; sun or light shade.

SNEEZEWEED (*Helenium autumnale*). To 6 feet with lemon-yellow to golden-yellow flowers with dark disks 2 inches across July to September. Hardy; sun.

SNOW TRILLIUM; WAKE ROBIN (*Trillium grandiflorum*). To 1½ feet with white to rosy pink flowers in May. Hardy; half shade; moist soil.

SOLOMON'S-SEAL (*Polygonatum multiflorum*). To 3 feet with greenish-white flowers in May, June. Hardy; shade.

SPEARMINT (*Mentha spicata*). To 2 feet with purplish, pink or white flowers in July, August. Hardy; sun or half shade.

SPIKE SPEEDWELL (*Veronica spicata*). To 1½ feet with blue, pink flowers in June, July. Hardy; half shade.

SPINY ACANTHUS (*Acanthus spinosus*). To 3 feet with dense purplish, erect flower spikes in July, August. Protect in North. Sun or light shade.

SPRENGER ASPARAGUS; ASPARAGUS FERN (*Asparagus Sprengeri*). To 6 feet with delicate, feathery foliage; pink, fragrant flower, bright red berry, winter blooming. Tender, shade to half shade.

SPRING MEADOW SAFFRON (*Bulbocodium vernum*). To 6 inches with violet-purple flowers in April. Semihardy bulb. In March, plant 3 inches deep, 3 inches apart. Protect in North.

SPRING SNOWFLAKE (*Leucojum vernum*). To 1 foot with white flowers tipped with green. Blooms in April. Hardy bulb. In September, plant 3 inches deep, 4 inches apart.

STAR OF BETHLEHEM (*Ornithogalum umbellatum*). To 1 foot with starlike, white, green-margined flowers in May, June. Hardy bulb; in September or October, plant 4 inches deep, 4 inches apart. Runs wild in North.

STIFF SUNFLOWER (*Helianthus rigidus scaberrimus*). From 3 to 8 feet with deep yellow, purple, or brown center to 3 inches across in September. Hardy; sun.

STOKES ASTER (*Stokesia laevis*). To 1½ feet with blue, purplish-blue flowers July to October. Hardy; sun.

STRIPED SQUILL (*Puschkinia scilloides var. libanotica*). To 1 foot with bluish flowers in April, May. Hardy bulb. In September, plant 3 inches deep, 3 inches apart.

SUMMER HYACINTH, GIANT (*Galtonia candicans*). To 4 feet with fragrant white flowers July to September. Semihardy bulb. In May, plant 6 inches deep, 18 inches apart. Moist soil. Protect in North.

SUNDROPS (*Oenothera fruticosa*). To 3 feet, with yellow flowers May to September. Hardy; half shade.

SUNDROPS, YOUNG'S (*Oenothera fruticosa var. Youngii*). To 3 feet, with yellow flowers in June, July. Hardy; half shade; dry soil.

SWEET VIOLET (*Viola odorata*). To 6 inches, with fragrant, deep-violet flowers in April, May. Hardy; half shade to shade.

TANSY (*Tanacetum vulgare*). To 3 feet, with yellow flowers in August, September. Hardy; sun or semishade.

TATARIAN CEPHALARIA (*Cephalaria tatarica*). To 6 feet with heads of creamy-white flowers July to September. Hardy; sun or light shade.

THRIFT (*Armeria maritima alba*). To 1 foot, with white flowers May to September. Hardy; sun.

VALERIAN; GARDEN HELIOTROPE (*Valeriana officinalis*). To 5 feet, with very fragrant, whitish, pinkish, lavender flowers in June, July. Hardy; sun or light shade; moist soil.

VIOLET BOLTONIA (*Boltonia latisquama*). To 6 feet, with blue-violet flowers in September, October. Hardy; sun or light shade. Moist soil.

VIOLET MONKSHOOD (*Aconitum Fisheri var. Wilsonii*). To 6 feet, with violet flowers July to September. Hardy; half shade.

VIRGINIA BLUEBELLS (*Mertensia virginica*). To 2 feet. Flowers with purple tube and blue bell in April. Hardy; shade to light shade.

VIRGINIA FALSE DRAGONHEAD (*Physostegia virginiana*). To 4 feet, with purplish-red to rose-pink, lilac flowers June to September. Hardy; part shade to sun; moist soil.

WHITE BOLTONIA (*Boltonia asteroides*). To 8 feet, with white to violet, purple flowers in August, September. Hardy; sun or light shade. Moist soil.

WHITE GLOBE TULIP (*Calochortus albus*). To 2 feet with white flowers with purplish base in June. Tender bulb. In September, plant 3 inches deep, 3 inches apart.

WHITE MUGWORT (*Artemisia lactiflora*). To 4 feet with white heads of loosely panicled flowers August to October. Best to protect in North; sun.

WHITELEAF EVERLASTING (*Helichrysum angustifolium*). To 1 foot. Foliage white-tomentose; flowers yellow in July, August. Semihardy; sun.

WILD SENNA (*Cassia marilandica*). To 4 feet, with yellow flowers in August, September. Hardy; sun; moist soil.

WILLOW OX-EYE (*Buphthalmum salicifolium*). To 2 feet, with yellow flowers in June, July. Hardy; sun.

YELLOW GENTIAN (*Gentiana lutea*). To 6 feet with citron-yellow flowers in July, August. Semihardy; sun; moist soil, cool conditions. Protect in North.

YELLOW WILD INDIGO (*Baptisia tinctoria*). To 4 feet with bright yellow flowers in June. Hardy; sun.

YUNNAN MEADOW RUE (*Thalictrum dipterocarpum*). To 2 feet with rose, lilac flowers in August, September. Hardy; sun or light shade.

Annuals

AFRICAN DAISY (*Arctotis stoechadifolia*). A summer favorite "daisy" from South Africa, easy to grow and drought resistant. The hybrids shown here have large blooms in cream, yellow, bronze, red; grow to 1 foot. The variety **Grandis** grows to 2 feet, has white flowers with violet blue disk and undersides. There are also good dwarf strains. CULTURE: Quick and easy from seed sown in open warm ground. Full sun; almost any kind of soil as long as it is well drained.

1. AFRICAN DAISY

ASTER; CHINA ASTER (*Callistephus chinense: see under Perennials Michaelmas Daisies*). Certainly one of the prettiest, most popular annuals. Graceful, colorful flowers on upright bushy stems 2 to 4 feet high. There are singles, doubles, crested, fluffed, fringed, or quilled with blooms to 4 inches across in colors from pure white, pale pink, rose, purple, navy-blue (**Burpeeana Bonnie Blue,** shown here, is one of the earliest to bloom, a clear medium blue), lavender, carmine, salmon, light blue, all but true orange, red, or yellow. Unfortunately equally inviting to many insects—do not plant in the same location year after year. CULTURE: Sun, any good soil, some shade tolerated.

2. ASTER (Burpeeana Bonnie Blue)

BABY BLUE EYES (*Nemophila Menziesii*). Low-growing hardy annual, only 6 to 8 inches high, with a profusion of large, lovely cup-shaped sky blue flowers, shading to white in the center (as **Insignis Blue,** shown here). Quick to grow and bloom; other colors include white (*N. alba*); white or pale blue with black center (*N. liniflora*); blue with white margins (*N. marginata*); pale blue, dotted purple or black (*N. atomaria*); brownish purple, edged white (*N. discoidalis*). Like sun or light shade, but not too much heat. In warm climates, best to sow seed in fall for spring bloom.

3. BABY BLUE EYES (Insignis Blue)

BABY'S BREATH (*Gypsophila elegans*). Annual Baby's Breath generally has showier though fewer flowers than perennial types. Two prominent colors—pure white, as **King of the Market,** shown here, with many graceful, very floriferous sprays, and **Rose,** a bright, rich rose. There are delicate pinks and pinky whites, too. Quick to come into bloom. CULTURE: Sun; although reputedly calcium soil-loving, will grow in any average soil.

4. BABY'S BREATH (King of the Market)

BACHELOR'S BUTTON; CORNFLOWER; RAGGED ROBIN; RAGGED SAILOR (*Centaurea cyanus*). An old popular favorite because of its ease of growth and gay flowers. Usually 2 to 2½ feet tall in typically bright blue (**Blue-Boy**); pale pink (**Pinkie**); deep lustrous red (**Red Boy**); and white (**Snowman**). Well-branched everblooming plants can be had by keeping all faded flowers promptly picked. Pretty dwarf doubles also available with **Jubilee** (large dark blue flowers), the All-American Winner (to 1 foot). CULTURE: Sun; easy and fast in any good soil; stands

5. BACHELOR'S BUTTON

heat and dry spells well. A hardy annual; may be sown in fall for early start in spring.

BALSAM (*Impatiens Balsamina: also see Rock Garden Plants*). A semiforgotten plant that deserves far more notice for its wealth of lovely flowers, its everblooming habits, its ease of culture, and most of all, for its

6. BALSAM (Double Camellia)

ability to bloom freely in fairly dense shade. Mine get but an hour or two of sun a day and are a mass of flowers all summer long. Colors: white, salmon, apricot, cerise, pink, rose, purplish red. Double camellia types, shown here, are probably the most elegant with large waxy bloom on sturdy, well-branched plants to 2 feet high. Most notable are the yellows; white striped with fuchsia; and rose. There are also dwarfs in pink, red, rose, white; extra dwarfs in purple, scarlet, whites, rose, all with large blooms. CULTURE: Easy in shade or sun, moist or dry soil. Seed pods interesting, pop open to spray seeds when ripe. Keep faded flowers pinched off for continuous bloom. Seed themselves freely.

CALIFORNIA POPPY (*Eschscholtzia californica*). Satiny, poppylike flowers; singles, semidoubles, doubles in gay glistening colors of pink, rose, white, golden yellow, dark reds. Forms dense, low growing mat of flowers 1 to 2 feet high. Very free blooming over a long period of time. Pretty, feathery blue-gray foliage. Often behaves as a perennial in warm climates. **Sweetheart** has unusually large, double flowers in brilliant rose; **Monarchs,** shown here, are semi-double in typical color range. Singles mostly in sunset range of pale yellows to deep red. CULTURE: Very easy in sun, and any good soil.

7. CALIFORNIA POPPY (Monarch)

CAPE DAISY; CAPE MARIGOLD; WINTER CAPE MARIGOLD (*Dimorphoteca aurantiaca*). Large daisylike flowers 3½ to 4 inches across in many pretty, clear colors: rose, white, apricot, light or deep yellows, deep salmon, golden orange. Grows 1 to 1½ feet tall. Seed sown in April

8. CAPE DAISY

generally produces flowers by June or July. In cool regions later sowing can produce blooms into October but Cape Daisies are usually grown as an early summer flower as they like it on the coolish side. CULTURE: Easy in any good but light soil, sun.

CHRYSANTHEMUM (*Chrysanthemum coronarium, C. carinatum: also see Perennials*). Hybrid summer chrysanthemums come in a great range of colors, singles, doubles, bicolors, tricolors, many zoned or

9. SUMMER CHRYSANTHEMUM

ringed in striking multicolored bands. Variously called **Crown Daisies, Painted Daisies** or just plain **Daisies.** All are of the easiest culture, blooming freely any time from July to September, depending on the strain. From 9 inches to 4 feet in height. CULTURE: Sun, any soil, preferably on the heavy side. Sow in early spring preferably where plants are to grow or in late fall for early spring start. Often seed themselves.

COCKSCOMB (*Celosia argentea cristata*). Multitudinous tiny flowers borne on bizarrely shaped clusters, crested or flattened, in spikes or plumes mostly in red, orange-red, pink, rose, yellow. **Toreador,** shown here, is a tall crested type with combs, 6 to 9 inches across, of brilliant red with scarlet

10. COCKSCOMB (Toreador)

highlights, green foliage. There are also dwarf crested types, giant-plumed and dwarf-plumed, all in typical color range. Bloom midsummer to frost. CULTURE: Easy to grow in sun; they like a light but rich moist soil.

COSMOS (*Cosmos bipinnatus, C. sulphureus*). A sturdy very free-flowering annual, easy to grow and able to withstand summer heat and drought—even poor soil. Rather slow to start into bloom, however, so start seeds early. Better yet, get the new earlier-blooming types as shown here. **Radiance Mammoth Sensation** begins to bloom 10 weeks from seed, continues blooming until frost, has giant, perfectly shaped blooms 4 to 6 inches across on robust plants 4 to 6 feet high. The fluted petals are a rich rose overlaid with crimson; the eye is golden. It is, of course, an All-American Silver Medal Winner. Other named colors are **Pink, Purity** (white), **Fiesta** (red and yellow), **Orange Flare** and **Yellow Flare;** doubles, singles, crested and fluted. Height averages 4 feet, although there are some dwarfs. CULTURE: Sun or part shade; prefer sandy average soil to rich. Pinch back young plants to produce more bushy plant. Seed themselves freely.

11. COSMOS (Radiance Mammoth Sensation)

FLOWERING TOBACCO; JASMINE TOBACCO (*Nicotiana*). Among the most fragrant and loveliest of flowers with long, tubular, star-shaped blooms in racemes on tall graceful stems. Many species, varieties, and hybrids, mostly opening at night and heavily perfuming the air. Colors white,

12. FLOWERING TOBACCO

red, yellow, lavender, purplish. Perennial in warm climates. *N. alata grandiflora* usually grown in the North. CULTURE: Does best in sun, warm soil. Slow to start if soil is cool, very rapid with warm weather. Sturdy, not fussy, stands drought well. Plants seed themselves freely.

FORGET-ME-NOT (*Myosotis alpestris*). Very pretty compact bushy plants (to 1 foot) with a profusion of brilliant, clear blue flowers. If sown early, will bloom in early spring. Unlike most forget-me-nots, these prefer a sunny location, well-drained soil.

13. FORGET-ME-NOT

GAY FLOWER (*Gaillardia amblyodon*). If you have plenty of sun, you can grow Gaillardias. Sturdy annuals from deep in the heart of Texas, they will take just about anything the summer has to offer—heat, drought, the doldrums. Bloom constantly June to November with large daisylike flowers, doubles or singles in yellow, red, sulphur orange, smoky reds often tipped in constrasting color, on sturdy, erect stalks to 5 feet. **Tetra Fiesta,** shown here, treated with colchicine has stronger, longer stems and brilliant smoke-red flowers tipped in yellow. CULTURE: Full sun, any well-drained soil.

14. GAY FLOWER (Tetra Fiesta)

HOLLYHOCK, ANNUAL (*Althea: see under Perennials and Biennials*). Although usually biennial, this strain will bloom the first year if seed is started early in spring. Colors, size, type of flowers, and culture are similar to biennial and semi-perennial types. Will often persist for several seasons and, of course, obligingly seeds itself freely as do all hollyhocks.

15. ANNUAL HOLLYHOCK

LARKSPUR (*Delphinium ajacis: see Delphinium under Perennials and Biennials*). One of the most graceful and decorative annuals with a much greater range of color than the perennial Delphinium species. Single or double flowers in sky-blue, dark blue, purple, blue reds, pink salmon, rose white; with new **Steeplechase Barcelona,**

shown here, a first and only bicolored blue and white. Plants average 3 to 4 feet in height with flowers on erect spikes. CULTURE: Full sun, average good to rich soil, but, to get good plants, seed must be started early as plants grow best during cool weather. Or you can plant seeds directly outdoors in late fall for early spring germination.

16. LARKSPUR (Steeplechase Barcelona)

LOBELIA (*Lobelia erinus*). A low-growing, bushy, compact annual highly prized for its profusion of shapely, bright blue flowers, some of spreading habit such as **Gracilis Blue** with ultramarine flowers (to 10 inches). **Mrs. Clibran Improved,** shown here, grows only 4 inches high constantly mounded with pretty, dark blue flowers with white eye. Other favorites are **Crystal Palace,** with dark-blue flowers, **Emperor William,** a sky-blue. Reddish types include **Prima Donna,** a maroon red. Good whites are **Snowball, White Lady, Snow Queen.** CULTURE: Easy to grow; likes some shade, particularly in hot climates; average good soil.

17. LOBELIA (Mrs. Clibran Improved)

MARIGOLD (*Tagetes*). Grow the new **Whitey** and if by any chance you get a pure white one you may win $10,000. For this is the prize offered by the Atlee Burpee Co. for the first true white marigold seed. Just about everything else has happened to these summer favorites including de-scenting—chrysanthemum-, peony- or carnation-flowered, singles, doubles, pygmies, dwarfs (see **Gypsy,** shown here, a dwarf double), intermediates, or giant-flowered as the **Giant Hybrid Climax** American marigold, also shown here (with flowers to 5 inches across). Colors are pale yellow, to yellow, to golden-orange-mahogany reds with the exception of the cream **Whitey,** which to date holds the most promise for the much coveted white. Needless to say marigolds have a long and fascinating history, both French and African types being natives of southwest America and Mexico. They are

18. MARIGOLD (Gypsy)

among the treasures Cortéz took back to Europe where their winning ways and bright colors made them a favorite offering to the Virgin Mary, therefore the name Mary's Gold. CULTURE: Sun, any good soil. Keep large-flowering types well watered. In general dwarfs are early to late summer bloomers; large are midsummer through fall bloomers.

19. MARIGOLD (Giant Hybrid Climax)

MIGNONETTE (*Reseda odorata*). Once grown chiefly for fragrance with rather nondescript yellowish flowers, mignonette is now available in the richest red imaginable on large colorful trusses as **Red Monarch,** shown here. A compact grower, very free blooming, deliciously scented. CULTURE: These do best in light shade, cool moist soil. Reputed not to transplant easily; best to sow outdoors where plants are to grow. Seed is very fine; be careful not to sow too thickly; thin plants promptly.

20. MIGNONETTE (Red Monarch)

NEMESIA; POUCHED NEMESIA (*Nemesia strumosa*). Varicolored white, yellow, orange, pink, crimson, scarlet, rose, blue, purple (to 2 feet). The low-growing hybrids, shown here, grow to only 12 inches, have exceptionally large, attractively shaped flowers. Often used as a pot plant. Will bloom over a long period of time, but prefer cool weather or cool climates. CULTURE: Sun or light shade; set rather close together since they tend to grow up rather than out.

21. NEMESIA

PAINTED TONGUE; VELVET FLOWER (*Salpiglossis sinuata*). Velvety, funnel-

22. PAINTED TONGUE

shaped, deep-throated flowers, probably the most luxuriously colored in the plant kingdom. Pungent reds, yellow golds, rich browns, purples, ivory on stems 1½ to 2½ feet tall, penciled, laced, and veined in gold. Bloom from July until frost. CULTURE: No special requisites as to soil; sun to light shade; start seeds early indoors, February or March if possible, for a long, prodigious blooming period.

PETUNIA (*Petunia*). Good news for petunia lovers . . . pelleted seeds, which increase the diameter of these elusive, dustlike particles about six times, are now available, thus making them infinitely more manageable. This just about removes the only drawback to the growing of these colorful plants. There are trailing and very dwarf types, popular for rock gardens or ground cover such as the trailer **Cheerful,** shown here, in varying shades of clear salmon, pink with dark rose veining, flowers almost 3 inches across. (All-American Bronze Medal Winner.) **Rosie,** shown here, new in 1961, an early dwarf, produces a mounded mass of deep rich rose flowers spreading to 2 feet across. Bedding petunias generally grow from 12 to 18 inches, may be trailing or bushy with single or double flowers in superb colors or color combinations. Some are exquisitely marked, starred, fringed, or frilled as **Giant Fringed Theodosea,** shown here, with blooms 4 to 5 inches across,

23. PETUNIA (Cheerful)

24. PETUNIA (Rosie)

bright rose with golden throat veined almost black. They display just about every color known except possibly a clear deep yellow and real sky-blue, bloom continuously throughout the summer. CULTURE: Sun or

25. PETUNIA (Giant Fringed Theodosea)

light shade and, except for double types which will not tolerate moist conditions, a moist soil suits them best. Although reputedly finicky to transplant I have never had any trouble. I *have* had trouble, however, in plants blooming themselves into increasingly smaller flowers, the result of pinching back and pruning to induce bushiness. This does indeed produce bushiness, and also many more blooms. The solution is to disbud (pinch off every other bud or so) thus producing fewer but better flowers. If possible, start seeds of large hybrids indoors in February through March; regular types March through April; outdoors from April on. Petunias are actually tender perennials grown as annuals in the North. They seed themselves freely but hybrids generally will not come true. Do not permit seed to form until the very end of blooming period or they will stop blooming.

PHLOX (*Phlox: see Moss Pink and Phlox Procumbens under Rock Gardens*). Most re-

26. PHLOX (Glamour Giant Tetra)

warding annuals and perennials, easy to grow, free and long flowering in a wide range of both brilliant and soft colors. Scarlet, vermilion, orange, red crimson, pale yellow, bright pink, white to near blue in a variety of heights and shapes. **Glamour Giant Tetra** (annual) has clusters of very large flowers, each 1¾ inches across—a clear light salmon with white eye (All-American Bronze Medal Winner), grows to 14 inches. The annual **Tetra Red,** to 20 inches, is similar in red with white and scented. There are also tall giants, tall or dwarf large-flowered strains, creepers and the very pretty starred and fringed types such as **Twinkle,** shown here, also an All-American Bronze Medal Winner. CULTURE: Sun, any good soil. Perennials can stand a little more shade; are easily propagated by division of clumps.

PINCUSHION FLOWER (*Scabiosa atropurpurea: see Scabiosa under Perennials and Biennials*). Fluffy, ball-shaped, 2½ to 3 inches across, these **Giant Imperial** hybrids have broad wavy petals, the typical "pincushion" centers. In white, cream peach,

27. PINCUSHION FLOWER

coral, bright pink, red, lavender, blue; grow to 3 feet on stiff stems. Medium-sized doubles grow to 2 feet with flowers 1½ to 2 inches, come in a very pretty color range . . . salmon pink, **Heavenly Blue** (All-American Bronze Medal Winner), maroon, blue, dark purple, yellow and tricolored blend of azure, white and pink. Dwarfs are also available. CULTURE: Full sun, any good soil.

PINKS (*Dianthus: see Pinks; Carnations; Sweet William under Perennials and Biennials and Sweet William under Annuals*).

28. PINK (Double Flowering Snowball)

Classified as annuals because they will bloom from July till frost if seed is sown in early spring. In mild climates, however, they may be treated as biennials. **Double Flowering Snowball,** shown here, looks much like a carnation with a profusion of large snowy white blooms, while the single **Floradales** are single flowered with deeply laciniated petals, brilliantly multicolored. Both are highly scented and grow to about 1 foot tall. Many other types are single or double with flowers 1 to 3 inches across in white, pink, rose, crimson, purple; self-colored, bicolored, multicolored, often with contrasting edges and eyes. CULTURE: Full sun, any good soil.

POT-MARIGOLD; CALENDULA (*Calendula officinalis*). Colorful, long-lasting flowers, old-fashioned favorites being typically orange, borne individually on 2-foot stems with rather sticky brittle leaves. Blooms over long summer period, often living over the winter in mild climates. New strains include semidouble to double types

29. POT-MARIGOLD (Apricot Beauty)

with flattened or quilled petals in pretty colors of cream, pale yellow, orange-red, pure orange with scarlet glow, a range of apricot tones; some bicolors. **Apricot Beauty,** shown here, is a double Pacific Beauty with bicolored apricot tones. **Orange Fantasy** is a clear bright orange prettily tipped or striped. CULTURE: Easy in any good average soil, sun.

RAINBOW DROPS; VISCARIA BLUE GEM (*Lychnis*). This dwarf strain has masses of light ultramarine blue flowers (1 to 1½ inches across) freely blooming

30. RAINBOW DROPS

throughout the summer on 8-inch-tall stems. To 8 inches with white, pink, or blue flowers. CULTURE: Sun, any good soil. Best to start seeds indoors in warm climates.

ROSE MOSS; SUN PLANT; SUN MOSS; WAX PINK (*Portulaca grandiflorum*). One of the sturdiest annuals, with brilliant colored flowers blooming from early summer until frost. Grows in any soil, withstands drought. With any attention at all, will form a dense carpet of color 4 to 6 inches high and is an excellent ground cover for sunny banks, between steppingstones, or to hide unsightly cracks and crevices. Flowers resemble waxed wild roses; doubles in lively pinks, scarlet, white, yellow and new peach tones, some striped with contrasting color; singles in orange, red,

31. ROSE MOSS

magenta, white, and buff. CULTURE: Full sun, any well-drained soil. Seeds itself profusely but doubles will not come true.

SATIN FLOWER (*Godetia grandiflora*). One of the few annuals to bloom in semishade. Unfortunately they also like a moist soil and temperatures on the cool side. A bushy plant, 12 to 15 inches, with silken flowers in combinations of pink, rose,

32. SATIN FLOWER

salmon, orange, red, orchid, white—singles or doubles, also pretty dwarf types. CULTURE: Half shade, any good soil, with moisture-retaining powers.

SHIRLEY POPPY (*Papaver Rhoeas*). These are the pretty descendants of the old Flanders Field poppy, just about as bright and gay and easy to grow as flowers come.

33. SHIRLEY POPPY (Double)

There are singles, doubles, prettily variegated, daintily frilled with papery silken petals. All in all as cheerful and showy a flower as exists. Colors: pale pinks, salmon, peach, apricot, terra-cotta, brilliant reds—doubles, shown here, often suffused with a second tint. Mostly vigorous, free-blooming branching plant 1½ to 3 feet tall. CULTURE: Easy. Sow early so they get a good start in cool weather. Full sun, average but well-drained soil. They self-sow freely; once you have them, you will have them forever.

SNAPDRAGON (*Antirrhinum majus*). Snapdragons are really half-hardy perennials sometimes surviving a mild winter—often with much greater display of flower—and surprising the northern gardener who thinks of them as annuals. New hybrids and colchicine-treated types are spectacular with tall flower spikes heavily laden with opulent blooms. **Sentinel,** shown here, carries some 100 flowers per spike with as

34. SNAPDRAGON (Sentinal)

many as 40 open at one time, grows to 3 feet tall; single flowers in crimson, deep yellow, pink, pale yellow, and bicolored orange-flushed rose. Giant ruffled tetraploids grow to about 2 feet with huge, fluffed blooms in yellow, deep crimson, shell pink, pungent rose, cream, and white. There are also rich doubles and bicolors. CULTURE: Sun or very light shade; fairly rich, well-drained soil. Will stand temperatures to freezing for brief periods but if well mulched will often carry over. For early bloom, start seeds indoors in March or April.

SPIDER PLANT (*Cleome spinosa* [*C. gigantea*]). **Pink Queen,** shown here (All-American Silver Medal Winner), is a bright salmon pink and is much too pretty, airy, and delicate to be called a spider. For all its fragile, graceful manners it is a robust grower—stands up very well under heat. Blooms from early June to late fall, up to 4 feet. Also in white or pink. CULTURE: Sun; any average soil.

35. SPIDER PLANT (Pink Queen)

STOCKS (*Mathiola*). Most familiar stocks are probably the night-scented (*M. bicornis*) with lavender blooms that open toward evening. Sturdy, very fragrant particularly after a rain, to 15 inches; bloom July through September. The **Giant Imperials,** shown here, are something else again with spikes to 2½ feet, heavily laden with double, very fragrant flowers in a rich range of colors: copper red, red, yellow, purple, pink, rose pink, white. There are also dwarf ten-week stocks and trisomic seven-week stocks in various pretty shades. CULTURE: Full sun, moderately rich soil. Start seed early indoors, if possible, so that all possible growth can be made during cool weather. During warm weather stocks grow luscious leaves but few blooms so give them a cool head start. After blooming, cut down stalk; at times they will bloom again in fall at the advent of cool weather.

36. STOCKS (Giant Imperial)

SUMMER FORGET-ME-NOT (*Anchusa capensis*). Bushy robust plants with clusters of tiny, bright gentian-blue flowers in graceful sprays on long stems. Very free-flowering from early summer until late fall. One of the few true blues in existence, **Blue Bird,** shown here, is an All-American Bronze Medal Winner, up to 18 inches. CULTURE: Plenty of moisture; very easy in any good soil, full sun. Actually a biennial but best treated as annual in cold regions. Will flower the first year if seed is started in April.

37. SUMMER FORGET-ME-NOT (Blue Bird)

SUNFLOWER (*Helianthus annuus vars.*). Recognize them? These are a far cry from the old super-sized yellow daisylike flowers we are all used to. Chrysanthemum-flowered, they are brilliant golden yellow with fat fluffy ball-like blooms 6 to 8 inches across, grow to 7 feet (although there are dwarf types, too). **Italian White** is a very pristine shade of white-to-creamy primrose with flowers to 3 inches across on 4-foot stems. Sturdy and easy to grow as all sunflowers. CULTURE: Sun, any average soil.

38. CHRYSANTHEMUM SUNFLOWER

SWEET ALYSSUM (*Lobularia maritima*). Quick, pretty, easy to grow, and very floriferous with **Carpet of Snow,** shown here, covering the ground thick as a carpet with multitudinous starchy white flowers (a dwarf to 4 inches). A new deep rose is **Rosie O'Day,** 1961 All-American Silver Medal Winner, low growing and covered with blooms. **Royal Carpet,** also an All-American Silver Medal Winner, grows only 2 to 3 inches high, about 10 inches across, massed with large heads of pure violet and singing purple. There is also a soft pink to lavender **Pink Heather** (All-American Bronze Medal Winner), a dwarf to 6 inches; and **Pinkie,** a pure white turning to pale pink with the advent of cool weather (to 6

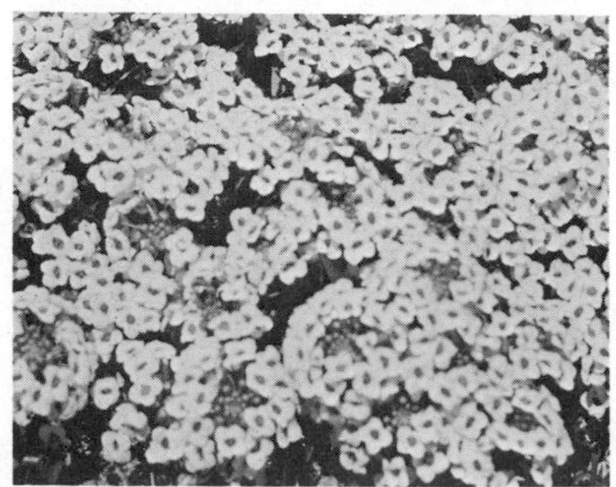

39. SWEET ALYSSUM (Carpet of Snow)

inches). Of delicious fragrance (to 8 inches) is **Sweet** with delicate white, honey-scented flowers. A superb robust taller strain (10 inches), **Tetra Snowdrift** has masses of large white everblooming flowers (the result of colchicine), excellent for cutting. Among the good violets is **Violet Queen,** with large, fragrant, bright flower clusters sometimes sprinkled with white. CULTURE: Quick and easy from seed, flowers in about 2 to 2½ months in any good soil, sun.

SWEET WILLIAM (*Dianthus barbatus: also see Perennials and Biennials*). Unlike the biennial Sweet Williams, these will bloom from seed the first year and are usually listed as annuals although they often will bloom a second year where winters are mild. An old-fashioned favorite with large brilliant clusters of phloxlike flowers. In many color combinations ranging from white to rose to red to purples; some starred or mottled; some with pure white eyes. Grows about 15 inches high. CULTURE: Full sun, any good soil. Plant seed in early spring for late summer and fall bloom.

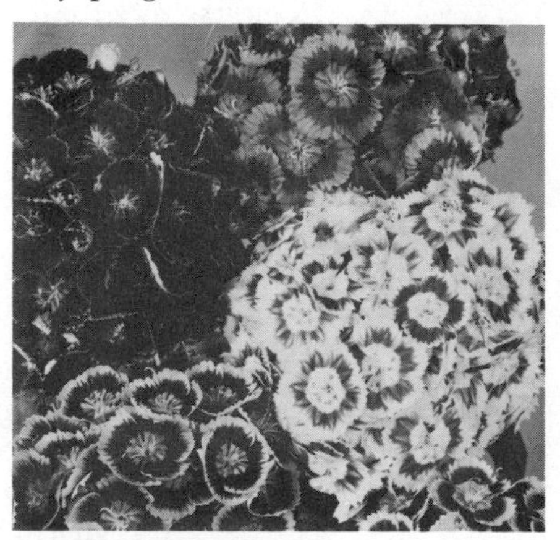

40. SWEET WILLIAM (Single)

VERBENA (*Verbena*). A most rewarding annual, behaving more like a perennial in the South (which indeed many are) with a long blooming period and a range of colors rivaled only by petunias. Flowers are borne on large trusses, each flower an inch or so across. Giants (*V. hortensis* hybrids) grow to 12 inches high, of spreading habit to 2½ feet across. **Floradale Beauty** comes in a range of perky pink to deep rosy red colors. **Lavender Glory** is a soft lavender with an eye the color of rich cream. **Spectrum Red**

is a clear vibrant red. All three are All-American Silver Medal Winners. There are also whites and pale coral pinks, yellows, and a new **Tetra Blue.** A pretty novelty is **Peppermint Stick** with red-striped white

41. VERBENA (Floradale Fancy)

blossoms. There are also dwarf compact verbenas (6 inches high—12 inches across). Tall erect ones (18 inches), dwarf erect ones (8 inches) in typical color range of white, pink, red, lavender, and purple. CULTURE: Full sun imperative. Seeds sown in late spring will not produce blooms until late July. The earlier you can sow indoors and *still give seedlings plenty of sun* the better. For most Northerners this is usually late March or April. In the South, late winter. Set out as soon as danger of frost is over. Plant tall varieties about 1 foot apart, dwarfs about 8 inches apart. Those of sprawling habit have semicreeping stems which often root, giving plant considerable spread as season goes on.

ZINNIAS (*Zinnias*). The **Burpeeana Giants,** shown here, are a lower, bushier (to 2 feet maximum), compact plant with blooms to 6 inches across. Gracefully quilled and ruffled petals in lovely colors and combinations of colors—bright orange, soft yellows, clear pinks, rose and corals, lavenders, pure white, sharp reds, vibrant purples. Zinnias today come in many different shapes, sizes, and colors, from tiny, dwarf pompon types to dahlia-flowered, to

42. ZINNIA (Burpeeana Giant)

fluffy and frilled giants—all in a remarkable range of colors. CULTURE: Full sun, any average soil, easy and quick from seed, very free blooming for a long period. Pinch back main flower stalk if you want a bushy plant.

More Annuals

(ALL BLOOM BEST IN THE SUN)

AFGHAN BLISTER CRESS (*Erysimum Perofskianum*). To 2 feet with yellow, orange flowers July to October.

BARTONIA (*Mentzelia Lindleyi*). To 4 feet with yellow flowers July to September.

BLUE LACE FLOWER (*Trachymene caerulea*). To 2 feet with blue flowers July to November.

BLUE LUPINE (*Lupinus hirsutus*). To 2 feet with blue-tipped white flowers in July, August.

BLUE TORENIA (*Torenia Fournieri*). To 1 foot with purple flowers with yellow centers, July to October.

BLUE-EYED MARY (*Collinsia verna*). To 2 feet with white, purplish flowers, blue lower lip, in May.

BRIDAL ROSE (*Matricaria inodora var. plenissima*). To 2 feet with orange-yellow, white flowers July to September.

BROWALLIA (*Browallia americana*). To 2 feet with blue, violet flowers in July, August.

CALLIOPSIS (*Coreopsis tinctoria*). From 1 to 3 feet with yellow flowers June to October.

CASTOR BEAN (*Ricinus communis*). To 15 feet (40 feet in the tropics) with showy foliage, panicles of flowers followed by long pods, June to September.

CHINESE FORGET-ME-NOT (*Cynoglossum amabile*). To 2 feet with blue flowers June to September.

CLARKIA (*Clarkia elegans*). To 3 feet with purple, rose, white flowers June to October.

CONEFLOWER (*Rudbeckia bicolor*). To 2 feet with yellow flowers with black disk July to September.

CORN POPPY (*Papaver Rhoeas*). To 3 feet with red, purple, scarlet, white flowers in August, September.

CUT-LEAVED MASK FLOWER (*Alonsoa incisifolia*). To 2 feet with scarlet, purple flowers, black throat, May to October.

DANDELION - LEAVED SUNDROP (*Oenothera acaulis*). 1 to 2 feet with white to bluish flowers June to October.

FLAXLEAF NAVELSEED (*Omphalodes linifolia*). 1 foot with white flowers July to September.

FLOSS FLOWER (*Ageratum conyzoides*). From 6 inches to 2 feet with blue, white flowers June to September.

FORKING LARKSPUR (*Delphinium Consolida*). To 1½ feet with blue, violet flowers July to September.

FOUR O'CLOCK (*Mirabilis Jalapa*). To 3 feet with red, yellow, white, striped flowers in August, September.

FRASER SUNDROP (*Oenothera glauca var. Fraseri*). From 2 to 3 feet with yellow flowers June to October.

GLOBE AMARANTH (*Gomphrena globosa*). To 1½ feet with various colored flowers in July.

HARTWEG LUPINE (*Lupinus Hartwegii*). To 3 feet with blue, part rose-colored flowers July to September.

HERB TREE MALLOW (*Lavatera trimestris*). To 6 feet with rose, red flowers July to September.

HINDU DATURA (*Datura Metel*). To 5 feet. Flowers white inside, purple to yellowish outside. Blooms in July.

HONESTY (*Lunaria annua*). To 1½ to 3 feet with white, purple flowers in June, July. Shade.

IMMORTELLE (*Xeranthemum annuum*). To 3 feet with white, purple, violet, and rose flowers in July.

JEWEL OF THE VELDT (*Ursinia anthemoides*). To 1 foot. Yellow flowers, purplish outside, June to September.

LANTANA (*Lantana Camara dwarf hybrids*). From 6 inches to 1 foot with variously colored flowers July to September.

LOVE IN A MIST (*Nigella damascena*). To 1½ feet with white, light blue flowers in July, August.

LOVE LIES BLEEDING (*Amaranthus caudatus*). From 3 to 5 feet with scarlet flowers June to August.

MEXICAN AGERATUM (*Ageratum Houstonianum*). To 2 feet with blue flowers May to October.

MEXICAN FIRE PLANT (*Euphorbia heterophylla*). To 3 feet with upper leaves blotched scarlet and white flower clusters, July to September.

MEXICAN POPPY (*Argemone mexicana*). To 3 feet with yellow or orange flowers, white-veined leaves. Blooms July to November.

POOR MAN'S WEATHERGLASS (*Anagallis arvensis var. caerulea*). To 6 inches with blue flowers May to October.

PROUD VENIDIUM (*Venidium fastuosum*). To 1½ feet. Orange flowers with purple-brown base, July to September.

ROCKET CANDYTUFT (*Iberis amara*). To 1 foot with white flowers June to September.

ROSE EVERLASTING (*Helipterum roseum*). To 2 feet. Flowers with rose or white bracts in August, September.

ROYAL SWEET-SULTAN (*Centaurea imperialis*). To 4 feet with white, rose, lilac, or purple flowers May to August.

SACRED DATURA (*Datura meteloides*). To 3 feet with white flowers tinged with rose or violet November to February. Good for West Coast. (Perennial grown as annual.)

SANVITALIA (*Sanvitalia procumbens*). To 6 inches. Yellow flowers with purple disk June to October.

SCARLET FLAX (*Linum grandiflorum var. coccineum*). To 1 to 2 feet with scarlet flowers in July, August.

SNOW-ON-THE-MOUNTAIN (*Euphorbia marginata*). To 2 feet with white flowers July to October.

SPINY AMBERBOA (*Amberboa muricata*). To 2 feet with pink, purple flowers in July, August.

STRAWFLOWER (*Helichrysum bracteatum*). To 3 feet with variously colored flowers July to September.

SUMMER ADONIS (*Adonis aestivalis*). To 1½ feet with crimson flowers in June, July.

SUMMER CYPRESS (*Kochia scoparia, var. trichophila*). From 1½ to 5 feet, grown for foliage which turns crimson in autumn. July to September.

SUMMER FIR (*Artemisia sacrorum, var. viridis*). To 10 feet of pyramidal growth with bright-green, much-dissected foliage; white, yellow flowers in August.

SUNSET HIBISCUS (*Hibiscus Manihot*). To 9 feet with yellow or whitish flowers to 9 inches across with dark brown center, in August, September. Moist soil. Sometimes perennial.

SWAN RIVER DAISY (*Brachycome iberidifolia*). To 1½ feet with blue, rose, and white flowers June to September.

SWEET PEA (*Lathyrus odoratus*). To 6 feet with variously colored flowers July to October. Moist soil.

TARWEED (*Madia elegans*). To 2 feet with yellow flowers July to September. For South only.

TASSEL FLOWER (*Emilia sagittata*). To 2 feet with red, scarlet flowers July to October. For South only.

TEXAN XANTHISMA (*Xanthisma texanum*). To 4 feet with yellow flowers July to September. For South only.

TOM THUMB NASTURTIUM (*Tropaeolum majus var. nanum*). Dwarf size with variously colored flowers July to October.

VIRGINIA STOCK (*Malcomia maritima*). To 1 foot with lilac, reddish to white flowers June to August.

WALKER'S SCHIZOPETALON (*Schizopetalon Walkeri*). From 6 inches to 1 foot with fragrant, fringed white flowers June to September.

WINGED EVERLASTING (*Ammobium alatum*). To 3 feet with yellow flowers in August, September.

WINGLEAF BUTTERFLY FLOWER (*Schizanthus pinnatus*). To 4 feet with variously colored flowers in July.

Rock Garden Plants

BALSAM, BUSH FLOWERED DWARF (Dwarf variety of *Impatiens Balsamina: see Balsam under Annuals*). Neat, tidy 8-inch "bushes" lavishly covered with waxy, double, camellialike blooms in salmon, cerise, pink, lavender, red, or white. Easy to grow; blooms freely from summer till frost in sun or part shade. An annual grown from seed.

1. BUSH FLOWERED DWARF BALSAM

BLUE CUP FLOWER (*Nierembergia caerulea*). Sometimes erroneously listed as *N. hippomanica.* Beautiful, large, lavender-blue or purple (as **Purple Robe,** shown here) cup-shaped flowers. Plants form low, compact, thick cover to 6 inches high. Semi-hardy perennial, best treated as an annual in severe climates. Will bloom from seed the first year or can be carried over by bringing plant indoors or by cuttings. Summer and fall blooming, likes sun and moisture.

2. BLUE CUP FLOWER (Purple Robe)

CALLIOPSIS (Dwarf *Coreopsis hybrids*). Gay decorative daisylike flowers in yellow, orange, red-browns and crimson, prettily marked and spotted. Grows 9 to 12 inches; blooms constantly from early summer till frost. Thrives in almost any soil; sun or part shade. An annual grown from seed.

3. CALLIOPSIS

CANDYTUFT (*Iberis*). Low-growing, ever-spreading hardy perennials or annuals with glossy, green foliage, excellent over stone walls. Masses of mostly pure white flowers in clusters, single or double; some fragrant. Among the perennials there are some very low shrubby types (*I. saxatilis*); some to 10 inches tall with snow-white flowers, evergreen foliage, **Edging Candytuft** (*I. sempevirens,* shown here); lilac-pink flowered *I. gibraltarica,* although marvelous for hot, dry places, need winter protection in the North. Among the annuals **Iceberg Hyacinth Flowered** (*I. coronaria*), shown here,

4. EDGING CANDYTUFT

5. ICEBERG HYACINTH FLOWERED CANDYTUFT

is among the showiest and tallest—much branched, each branch topped with snowy-white spikes of bloom. Most of the colored Candytufts are also annuals (*I. umbellata*), come in carmine, pink, lilac, rose, purple, and white, and are among the sturdiest and most easily grown. They are great favorites for city gardens. All like sun or very light shade and stand dryness well. PROPAGATION: Perennials—cuttings in fall, seed, division. Annuals—seed.

CARPATHIAN BELLFLOWER (*Campanula carpatica*). Hardy perennial, low

6. CARPATHIAN BELLFLOWER

growing (8 to 12 inches), well-branched mounds covered with large, open, blue, lavender, mauve, or white bell- or cup-shaped flowers 1 inch across. Sun or semi-shade. Blooms July to September. PROPAGATION: Division.

CELOSIA (DWARF FEATHERED) (*Celosia argentea cristata: see Cockscomb under Annuals*). **Firefeather,** shown here, is a dwarf bushy plant; has branches tipped with fiery-red silken plumes. Annual grown from seed; likes sun and any good moist

7. CELOSIA (Firefeather)

soil. Strain **Golden Feather** is a deep yellow. Blooms from midsummer until frost. PROPAGATION. Seed.

FAN COLUMBINE (DWARF WHITE) (*Aquilegia flabellata nana-alba: see Columbine under Perennials*). Hardy perennial with large, pure white flowers on 8- to

8. FAN COLUMBINE

12-inch stalks, flat, fan-shaped leaves. Blooms in May; sun or light shade. PROPAGATION: Seed or division.

CYCLAMEN (DWARF, HARDY) (*Cyclamen Atkinsii*). One of the prettiest of the hardy cyclamen, a hybrid with either snow-white flowers as *album* shown here, or pink, both marked in red. The leaves

9. CYCLAMEN (Album)

are spotted silvery white. Enchanting plants for woodland or light to semishaded location. These plants like rich woodsy moisture-retaining soil with good drainage. PROPAGATION: Tubers. Plant 1 inch deep. Seed: takes only a year to come into bloom.

FLOSS FLOWER (DWARF) (*Ageratum*). A favorite annual for nooks and crannies. **Tetra Blue Mink,** shown here, is particu-

10. FLOSS FLOWER (Blue Mink)

larly vigorous, has large fluffy blue flowers which eventually cover the dwarf, compact plant 6 to 8 inches high with 1-foot spread. Other colors in various shades of blue; also pure white. Grows in any good soil, sun or part shade.

FORSYTHIA; GOLDEN BELLS DWARF HYBRID (*Forsythia viridissima Bronxsensis: see also Shrubs, Trees, Hedges*). An excellent hardy low shrub (only 12

11. FORSYTHIA

inches high) for the rock garden, recently developed by the Bronx Botanical Gardens. Masses of typical "golden bells" borne on graceful, arching branches before the leaves appear. Good foliage all summer. Easy in sun or light shade. PROPAGATION: Cuttings.

FRINGED BLEEDING HEART (*Dicentra eximia: see Bleeding Heart under Perennials*). Hardy perennial to 2 feet with racemes of small, pendulous pink or rose

12. FRINGED BLEEDING HEART

"hearts," attractive feathery foliage. Likes light fertile soil; sun or light shade. Blooms May to July. PROPAGATION: Division of crown or roots.

GEUM (*Geum* or *Avens*). Hardy perennial, a natural for rock gardens with low, leafy mounds of strawberrylike leaves, single or double flowers, sometimes clustered. *Geum*

13. GEUM (Mrs. Bradshaw)

Borisii is a hybrid runner—small, low growing (to 8 inches) with brilliant orange-yellow flowers; blooms May to July and again in September. **Mrs. Bradshaw,** shown here, grows to 15 inches; has double flowers in bright scarlet; blooms all summer; and is more typically a "border perennial." Sun or light shade; loose rich gravelly soil. Grows rapidly. PROPAGATION: Division (every 2 years or so).

GLOBE-FLOWER (*Trollius europaeus*). Hardy perennial with large round citron-

14. GLOBE-FLOWER

yellow flowers borne singly on 18- to 24-inch stems, decorative foliage. Grows in clumps, usually in damp places. Blooms late spring into summer. Likes rich, moist soil; sun or part shade. PROPAGATION: Seeds; division.

GOLDEN-TUFT; GOLD-DUST; BASKET OF GOLD (*Alyssum saxatile*). Hardy perennial with masses of golden-yellow flowers clustered on much-branching stems. Forms a thick spreading mat on the ground or covers cracks and crevices on rock walls. The variety *flore-pleno,* shown here, has double flowers, grows to 1 foot; *compactum* has single flowers, is somewhat lower growing; *citrinum* has lemon-yellow flowers. This perennial likes sun; and loose, well-drained soil. Blooms April to June. PROPAGATION: Seed; cutting; root division.

15. GOLDEN-TUFT

HENS AND CHICKENS (*Sempervivum tectorum*). Hardy perennial, a great favorite both for its prolific progeny and spreading habit and its ability to grow practically on stone. Succulent rosettes 3 to 4 inches across; tiny pinkish-red flowers (if and when it blooms). Requires sun; withstands dryness. PROPAGATION: Automatic, by offsets.

16. HENS AND CHICKENS

IRIS, DWARF WHITE *(Iris cristata alba; see Iris under Perennials)*. Clear white blooms on very short stems; typically flat, sword-shaped leaves. Hardy perennial, spring blooming. Sun or part shade. PROPAGATION: Division of rhizomes.

17. DWARF WHITE IRIS

JACOB'S-LADDER; GREEK VALERIAN, CHARITY (*Polemonium caeruleum*). Very floriferous, hardy perennial with many clusters of nodding bright-blue flowers on slender stems; grows to 3 feet. Variety *alba* has white flowers; *himalayanum* has lavender-blue flowers. Quick to grow and to spread by seeding itself. Blooms spring into summer; sun or light shade. PROPAGATION: Division; seed.

18. JACOB'S-LADDER

LONG-SPURRED BARRENWORT *(Epimedium grandiflorum, E. macranthum)*. Hardy perennial with spreading clusters of dainty flowers in white (*album, niveum*), rose (*roseum*), violet (*violaceum*); pretty heart-shaped leaves. Grows to 9 inches. Ideal for cool shady spots, as a ground cover or among rocks. Semishade; blooms in May. PROPAGATION: Division.

19. LONG-SPURRED BARRENWORT

MARIGOLD, DWARF (*Tagetes hybrids: see Marigold under Annuals*). These Burpee pygmy doubles have fluffy, ball-like blooms 1½ inches across, borne on compact plants 6 to 8 inches tall. Bloom from early summer till frost. Colors: red-mahogany; gold, flecked red; primrose yellow; lemon yellow; sometimes with centers of other colors. Easy to grow in a sunny location in any good soil. An annual grown from seed.

20. DWARF MARIGOLD

MONARCH ROCK CRESS (*Aubrieta deltoidea grandiflora*). Hardy perennial, spreads to form thick carpet of color covering crevices, cracks, etc. Dwarf bushy com-

21. MONARCH ROCK CRESS

pact; grows anywhere from 2 to 10 inches high, covered with rose, lilac, or deep-violet flowers. Thrives in sun or half shade; blooms April, May. Apt to be short lived in hot climates; best to treat as biennial and keep new plants coming along. PROPAGATION: Division of clumps; seed; cuttings.

MOSS PINK; GROUND PINK; ROCK PHLOX (*Phlox subulata: see Phlox procumbens in this section and Phlox under Annuals*). Most widely known and grown of rock-garden Phloxes. In spring, smothered by blooms of many excellent colors—white, pale pink, rose pink, red, mauve, lavender, salmon, pale blue, often with deeper colored eye. Excellent where low mats of massed color desired; also good as ground cover after blooming, with rich green foliage (sometimes evergreen in mild climates). Perennial to 6 inches. Blooms

22. MOSS PINK

best in full sun, dryish soil. Spreads rapidly. PROPAGATION:Best to root cuttings; also from seeds but color not always predictable.

NASTURTIUM, DWARF DOUBLE (*Tropaeolum majus*). Easy and fast growing, producing masses of flowers from summer till frost. To 1 foot high, spreading 1½ feet across. Giant double or semi-double blooms, sweetly scented, in cherry-rose, golden yellow, sharp orange, pale yellow, scarlet. Full sun for full bloom. Dryish, sandy, or gravelly soil, rather poor in nutrients, produces the best flowers. A tender perennial, very sensitive to frost, usually grown as an annual. PROPAGATION: Seeds; cuttings.

23. DWARF DOUBLE NASTURTIUM

PHLOX PROCUMBENS (*See Moss Pink in this section and Phlox under Annuals*). A hybrid of somewhat dubious parentage, reputed to be a cross between **Creeping Phlox** (*P. stolonifera*) and **Moss Pink** (*See in this section*) (*P. subulata*) and often grown as *P. amoena* (which it is not). What it *does* have is very pretty, typically phlox-like flowers, blooming in spring in great profusion. Colors: violet, soft blue (*caerulea*), rose-pink (*rosea*). Hardy perennial to 1 foot; requires sun. PROPAGATION: Division, cuttings.

24. PHLOX PROCUMBENS

POLYANTHA PRIMROSE (*Primula polyantha*). Hardy perennial 6 to 9 inches high,

25. POLYANTHA PRIMROSE

spring-flowering, with large blooms in white, cream, pale yellow, pink, rose, orange, lilac, purple, red, often bicolored. Ideal for naturalizing in woodlands. For partial shade; will also endure sun if soil is kept rich and moist. In mild climates may bloom all winter. Likes cool, moist, shady locations. PROPAGATION: Seed, but slow to germinate. Division (best right after flowering).

SEA PINK; THRIFT (*Armeria*). Attractive, much hybridized, hardy perennial of low-tufted growth, blooming from early spring through late summer. **Sutton's Giant Pink,** shown here, has bright rose pink blossoms 2 inches across on wiry stems rising 1 to 1½ feet above matlike plants. Other colors are in the pale pink through rose, coral to red range. Sea Pinks like light dryish soil; full sun. PROPAGATION: Seed; cuttings.

26. SEA PINK (Sutton's Giant Pink)

SNOW IN SUMMER (*Cerastium tomentosum*). Hardy perennial to 6 inches;

27. SNOW IN SUMMER

creeping matlike with a profusion of glistening white starlike flowers, white woolly foliage. Ideal for dry, sunny, rocky locations, banks, tree stumps, etc. Blooms May and June. PROPAGATION: Division; cuttings; seeds.

SNOWDROP (*Galanthus*). Early spring-flowering, hardy bulbs, ideal for rock gar-

28. SNOW DROP

dens or naturalizing. Charming, drooping, snow-white flowers, green straplike leaves (6 to 12 inches high). Plant in September, 3 inches deep, some 2 to 4 inches apart. Can be left a long time without disturbing. PROPAGATION: Division of clumps. Give winter protection in severe climates.

SPANISH BLUEBELL (*Scilla hispanica, S. campanulata*). Hardy perennial; one of

29. SPANISH BLUEBELL

the most charming of the early spring-flowering bulbs; with nodding bells strung on strong, tall spikes, 12 to 15 inches high.

Lovely colors and many named varieties such as: **Azalea,** a brilliant pink; **King of the Blues,** a true, bright sky-blue; **Heavenly Blue,** a delicate porcelain blue. **Peach Bloom,** pink; **Mt. Everest,** white. Easy to grow, can be left undisturbed for years. Most effective grown in clumps among ferns (to hide wilting foliage) under trees. Plant 3 inches deep, 3 inches apart in sun or shade. PROPAGATION: Division as soon as leaves die down.

SPRING SNOWFLAKE (*Leucojum vernum*). Hardy, early spring-flowering bulbs

30. SPRING SNOWFLAKE

with very beautiful, drooping, white-tipped green flowers. Likes sandy loamy soil; sun. Plant in early September or even late August—about 6 inches apart, 2 or 3 inches deep. PROPAGATION: Division, as soon as the leaves have died down and before new growth starts.

STRIPED SQUILL (*Puschkinia scilloides*). Very beautiful spring-flowering bulbs—a great favorite for rock gardens. Flowers,

31. STRIPED SQUILL

icy blue-white striped in porcelain blue, are carried in clusters on tall spikes. Easy to grow, thrives in any average soil in a sunny location. Plant bulbs in fall. PROPAGATION: Divide every 2 to 3 years.

SWEET WOODRUFF (*Asperula odorata*). Rapidly spreading plant useful for shady places and under trees, covered with

32. SWEET WOODRUFF

mounds of tiny white flowers in spring; lanceolate leaves. Hardy perennial, to 8 inches. Leaves are fragrant when cut and dried. Likes semishade, moist soil. PROPAGATION: Seeds; division of roots and clumps.

WINTER ACONITE (*Eranthis hyemalis*). Hardy tuberous perennial; ideal to tuck

33. WINTER ACONITE

among rocks or in woodland for early spring bloom. Usually grows only 3 or 4 inches high with large buttercup-yellow flowers; ruffled green leaves. Often appears in the snow in early spring. Plant tubers immediately upon receiving in late August to early September, 2 inches deep, 2 inches apart. Likes well-drained, moist situations; light to semishade. PROPAGATION: Division of roots.

WOOD ANEMONE (*Anemone blanda*). Hardy perennial, with masses of brilliant sky-blue flowers, grown from tuberous roots. The variety *scythinica* is white, tinted blue outside; *rosea* is rose-pink. Thrives in any good loose soil with a little added leafmold; sun or shade. Flowers in early spring; low growing; excellent for naturalizing in woodland or among rocks. Plant roots in September about 2 inches deep. PROPAGATION: Root division in early spring.

34. WOOD ANEMONE

More Rock Garden Plants

(ALL PERENNIAL; SUN OR LIGHT SHADE UNLESS OTHERWISE NOTED)

ALPINE SKULLCAP (*Scutellaria alpina*). To 10 inches. Flowers: purple, white, and pale yellow, July to September. United States.

ALPINE TOADFLAX (*Linaria alpina*). To 6 inches. Flowers: blue with orange palate, July, August. United States.

AMERICAN MAIDENHAIR FERN (*Adiantum pedatum*). From 8 inches to 1½ feet. Dainty evergreen foliage. Requires winter protection in the North. Shade.

CHECKERED LILY (*Fritillaria meleagris*). To 1½ feet. Flowers: "checkered" purple or maroon, April, May. Half shade. Good in the North.

COMMON THYME (*Thymus vulgaris*). To 8 inches. Flowers: lilac, purple, May, June. United States.

CORAL BELLS (*Heuchera sanguinea*). To 2 feet. Flowers: red, June to September. United States.

CREEPING GYPSOPHILA (*Gypsophila repens*). To 6 inches. Flowers: white, pink, June, July. United States.

CUSHION PINK (*Silene acaulis*). To 2 inches. Flowers: reddish purple, May to August. Requires half shade. United States.

DWARF POLEMONIUM (*Polemonium humile*). To 9 inches. Flowers: blue, purple, June, July. United States.

FLESH COLORED ROCK JASMINE (*Androsace carnea*). To 3 inches. Flowers: pink, whitish with yellow eye, in July. Requires winter protection in North.

GOLDMOSS (*Sedum acre*). To 3 inches. Flowers: yellow, May to August. United States.

ICE PLANT (*Cryophytum crystallinum*). To 6 inches. Flowers: white to pink to rose, in August. Good for West Coast.

ICELAND POPPY (*Papaver nudicaule*). To 1 foot. Flowers: orange, yellow, white or red, April to July; August to October. Good in the North.

INDIA ASTER (*Aster subcaeruleus*). To 1 foot. Flowers: light blue, July to September. United States.

MAIDEN PINK (*Dianthus deltoides*). From 4 to 12 inches. Flowers: red, pink with scarlet eye, May, June. Good in the North.

MOUNTAIN AVENS (*Dryas octopetala*). To 4 inches. Flowers: white, in June. Requires winter protection in the North.

MOUNTAIN SANDWORT (*Arenaria montana*). To 4 inches. Flowers: white, May, June. United States.

MYRSINITES-LIKE SPURGE (*Euphorbia Myrsinites*). To 1 foot. Flowers: yellow, April, May. United States.

NARBONNE FLAX (*Linum narbonense*). To 2 feet. Flowers: bright sky-blue with white eye, May, June. United States.

PASQUE FLOWER (*Anemone Pulsatilla*). To 1 foot. Flowers: blue, magenta, violet, in April. United States.

PINK SAND VERBENA (*Abronia umbellata*). To 6 inches. Flowers: magenta, in April. United States.

ROCK ASTER (*Aster alpinus*). To 10 inches. Flowers: blue, red-purple, May, June. United States.

ROCK SOAPWORT (*Saponaria ocymoides*). To 9 inches. Flowers: pink, May to August. United States.

ROCK SPEEDWELL (*Veronica fruticulosa*). To 6 inches. Flowers: blue, pink, May, June. United States.

ROSY THRIFT (*Statice Armeria var. Laucheana*). To 1 foot. Flowers: rose, May to August. United States.

SEA-LAVENDER (*Limonium eximium; Goniolimon eximium*). To 2 feet. Flowers: lilac-rose, in August. Good for coastal regions.

SHOWY STONECROP (*Sedum spectabilis*). To 1½ feet. Flowers: pink, August, September. United States.

SILVER-LEAVED CRANESBILL (*Geranium argenteum*). To 5 inches. Foliage: pink with darker veins, June, July. Good in the North.

SPRING ADONIS (*Adonis vernalis*). To 1½ feet. Flowers: yellow, April to June. United States.

STILLMAN COREOPSIS (*Coreopsis Stillmanii*). To 1 foot. Flowers: yellow, June, July. Annual. United States.

STRIPED SQUILL (*Puschkinia scilloides*). To 1 foot. Flowers: blue, April, May. Good in the North.

SUN ROSE (*Helianthemum nummularium*). To 1 foot. Flowers: yellow, June, July. Requires winter protection in the North.

TRUE FORGET-ME-NOT (*Myosotis scorpioides var. semperflorens*). To 8 inches. Flowers: blue, white, yellow, or pink centers, June to August. Shade. Good in the North.

TUBE CLEMATIS (*Clematis heracleaefolia*).From 2 to 4 feet. Flowers: blue, August, September. United States.

VARIEGATED MEADOW SAFFRON (*Colchicum variegatum*). To 3 inches. Flowers: rose, September, October. United States.

WALL ROCK CRESS (*Arabis albida*). To 1 foot. Flowers: white, April to June. United States.

YELLOW-EYE BUTTERCUP (*Ranunculus amplexicaulis*). To 1 foot. Flowers: white, May, June. Half shade. United States.

Trailers, Ground Covers, Creepers

BUGLEWEED; CREEPING BUGLE (*Ajuga reptans*). Hardy herbaceous perennial. An excellent creeper and rapid grower forming a thick, low, dense carpet of glossy dark-green or purplish or variegated leaves. Myriad perky spikes to 9 inches of bright blue-purple, pink, or white flowers in spring (watch it, some of the white or pink sold may be *A. genevensis* which does not creep). Of simple culture, does best in rich moist soil with semishade, but can stand sun, shade, even dense shade if it receives sun

1. BUGLEWEED

some part of the day. Set plants 8 or 9 inches apart, will grow out from all directions. PROPAGATION: Easy from stem cuttings in water; division in spring; seed.

CINQUEFOIL (*Potentilla*). Hardy shrubby perennials, great favorites for rock gardens and as ground covers. The variety *fruticosa mandshurica,* shown here, is low growing (6 inches high) with small grayish, silken leaves, very deeply cut; is covered with white flowers in early spring. The variety *verna-nana* is very dwarf (only 2 inches high); forms a thick, dense, tufted mat of dark green leaves and is a solid sheet of golden flowers in April or May. An excellent rock-wall plant, too. Easy to grow in

2. CINQUEFOIL

any good soil (a little on the alkaline side if possible). Sun. PROPAGATION: Seeds, division, cuttings (often preferred).

CREEPING MADAGASCAR PERIWINKLE (*Vinca rosea hybrid: see Periwinkle*

3. CREEPING MADAGASCAR PERIWINKLE (Rose Carpet)

under Perennials and Biennials). **Rose Carpet,** shown here, is a tender perennial grown as an annual in cold climates. Of rapid creeping habit, covering a 2-foot circle at maturity. Grows only 4 to 6 inches high massed with rose blossoms; glossy green leaves. Stands shade and heat. Looks fresh and cool when everything else is drying up. PROPAGATION: Seeds; cuttings.

ENGLISH IVY (*Hedera helix vars.*). Hardy perennial, a classic ground cover or climber with thick, leathery, glossy evergreen leaves

4. ENGLISH IVY

forming a dense luxuriant carpet. The plant spreads or climbs by long trailers which root to the ground or attach themselves to walls as the case may be. Excellent under trees or other shady location. Will also thrive in full sun if ground is kept moist. PROPAGATION: Easy from cuttings 6 to 9 inches long even in water.

GRAPE HYACINTH (*Muscari*). Hardy bulbous perennial with masses of bright

5. GRAPE HYACINTH

bluish-purple flowers on spikes that bloom in early spring—6 to 12 inches high. Excellent for naturalizing or carpeting near shrubs. Of easy culture, spreads rapidly by offsets and by self-seeding. **Heavenly Blue** (*M. armeniacum*) is perhaps the most brilliant grape hyacinth. There are also some blue, pink, and white forms (*M. botryoides*). Needs sun. PROPAGATION: Bulbs. Plant late summer or early fall to establish plants properly for early spring bloom. Do not worry if they start to grow—they should. Plant 2 inches deep, 3 inches apart.

JAPANESE SPURGE; PACHYSANDRA (*Pachysandra terminalis*). Hardy evergreen perennial, one of the most reliable ground covers for semishady places. Spreads by branching rootstocks. Forms dense, green carpeting winter and summer. Not fussy about soil; likes moisture. PROPAGATION: Division in spring; stem or root cuttings in summer.

6. JAPANESE SPURGE

LILY OF THE VALLEY (*Convallaria majalis*). Hardy perennial with tiny, white,

7. LILY OF THE VALLEY

nodding fragrant bells strung on individual stems. Excellent ground cover for shady places, thriving in rich moist soil. Can be left undisturbed for many years; spreads rapidly through underground runners. Best time to plant in September or October; put pips 1 inch underground, 3 inches apart. Blooms in early spring. Variety *rosea* has pinkish double flowers; *variegata* has variegated leaves. *Fortunei,* shown here, has the largest leaves and flowers of all.

PERIWINKLE; MYRTLE (*Vinca minor*). Hardy evergreen perennial (about 6 inches) with glossy green leaves, pretty single or double blue, lavender-blue, or white

8. PERIWINKLE

flowers; also variegated varieties. One of the finest ground covers, forming long trailing stems that root quickly, thus spreading to dense green carpet. Sun, semishade, or shade; thrives in almost any soil but does best in moist soil. PROPAGATION: Stem cuttings in late summer or fall; division in early spring.

PLANTAIN LILY (*Hosta* often called *Funkia*). Hardy perennial; excellent ground cover (clumps to 1½ to 3 feet) for moist shady locations. Many good species and varieties: Short-cluster **Plantain Lily** (*H. Sieboldiana*) has bluish-green foliage, white purple-tinged flowers. **Blue Plantain Lily** (*H. caerulea*) has dark-green foliage, lavender-blue flowers. Handsomely variegated types are: **Wavy-Leaved Plantain Lily** (*H. undulata*)—green leaves lavishly brushed with white, pale lavender flowers. **Narrow-Leaved Plantain Lily** (*H. lancifolia albo-*

9. PLANTAIN LILY

marginata)—slender green leaves, margined white, lavender flowers. **Tall-Cluster Plantain Lily** (*H. Fortunei variegata*)—pronounced cream-white variegated leaves. All are spring to early summer blooming with the exception of the **Fragrant Plantain Lily** (*H. plantaginea*) which bears fragrant white flowers in late summer or autumn; green leaves. PROPAGATION: Best by division of clumps; sometimes seed.

VERBENA; VERVAIN (*Verbena rigida; V. venosa*). Half-hardy perennial treated as an annual in cold regions as it blooms from seed sown outdoors the first year. Of spread-

10. VERBENA

ing habit, to 1 foot, with spikes of bright red-purple, white, or lilac flowers. A profuse bloomer from July until frost. Likes sun, any good soil. PROPAGATION: Seeds; cuttings.

VIOLETS (*Viola species*). Hardy perennials—one of the loveliest ground covers for shady locations with myriad blooms in early spring. Many species and varieties with flowers in white, lavender, mauve, pink, violet, red, purple, even yellow—many fragrant. Violets spread quickly by runners and by self-sowing (although some do not produce seeds). Dig up and divide plants intermittently to give them more elbow room. They will reward you with larger, more lavish bloom. Like shade and moisture, woodsy soil. Will not tolerate much sun. PROPAGATION: Division; seed (with some).

11. VIOLET

WANDERING JEW (*Tradescantia fluminensis vars.*). Tender perennial with trailing stems of green or variegated leaves

12. WANDERING JEW

striped white (*albo-vittata*) or yellow (*aurea*); unimportant white flowers. (The red-tinged-leaved Wandering Jews are *Zebrina pendula* often listed as *Tradescantia laekenensis*). Excellent for ground cover in the South, often grown as house plant in the North. Of the easiest culture in almost any moist soil; semishade, even deep shade. Spreads rapidly rooting itself as it goes. Cannot stand too much sun. PROPAGATION: Very easy from cuttings, even in water; division.

More Trailers, Ground Covers, Creepers
(ALL PERENNIAL)

ALLEGHANY PACHYSANDRA (*Pachysandra procumbens*). Hardy, deciduous trailer and ground cover with spreading clumps of leaves larger than the usual types. Also good in the rock garden. Shade.

ALPINE CATCHFLY (*Silene alpestris*). Dwarf deciduous ground cover useful for rockeries; glistening white flowers June to August.

AMERICAN TWINFLOWER (*Linnaea borealis var. americana*). Hardy, miniature, evergreen ground cover useful for boggy, woodsy soils in cool sections of the country. Flowers bell-shaped, fragrant in rose, white; fruit, yellow. Blooms spring to early summer. Semishade, moist soil.

BABY WINTERCREEPER (*Euonymus radicans var. minimus*). Good, hardy, evergreen ground cover. Unimportant flowers in May; pretty, pinkish fruit.

BISHOP'S HAT (*Epimedium grandiflorum*). Excellent hardy ground cover with foliage turning beautiful bronze in fall, persisting until winter. Thrives in part shade, moist, well-drained soil. Good under evergreens. Bears red, violet, or white flowers in May, June.

BLACK-EYED SUSAN (*Thunbergia alata*). Tender deciduous ground cover or vine grown as annual in the North. Showy, cream-yellow flowers with dark-purple throat, June to October. (*See under Vines and Climbers.*)

BOX HUCKLEBERRY (*Gaylussacia brachycera*). Semihardy, outstandingly good ground cover for under white pines and rhododendrons. Hardy to Massachusetts. Evergreen; white or pink flowers in mid-May.

CHAMAEDRYS GERMANDER (*Teucrium Chamaedrys*). Semihardy, good, compact, low-growing plant with purplish or rose flowers in summer. Can be sheared to even bushier shape. Hardy to Massachusetts.

CLIMBING HYDRANGEA (*Hydrangea petioloris*). Hardy vigorous climber or creeper, although a slow starter. Unsurpassed for camouflaging a pile of rocks or what-have-you. Best of all, it covers without throttling. Very handsome when allowed to climb up a tree. Flowers in large white clusters, mid-June.

COMB SPEEDWELL (*Veronica pectinata*). Dwarf, hardy, deciduous trailer useful in the rock garden. Flowers: deep blue with white center, in May.

CORSICAN SANDWORT (*Arenaria balearica*). Semihardy evergreen ground cover particularly good for shade. Tiny, mossy, forms solid, sodlike carpet. Bears white flowers March to August. Hardy to Massachusetts.

CREEPING BLUETS (*Houstonia serpyllifolia*). Dense, grasslike, hardy ground cover—a thick carpet of deep blue flowers June to August.

CREEPING CHARLIE; MONEYWORT (*Lysimachia Nummularia*). Hardy deciduous trailer and ground cover, ideal for under trees or in low, wet areas. Likes shade and moisture. Yellow flowers, June to August.

CREEPING COTONEASTER (*Cotoneaster adpressa*). Hardy deciduous trailer and ground cover of graceful dense habit, with short, stiff, low branches. Bears white or pinkish blossoms in June, followed by red fruit. Very pretty, ornamental. Likes sun.

CREEPING HOLLY GRAPE (*Mahonia repens*). Hardy evergreen ground cover with yellow flowers in May, followed by dark-blue, grapelike fruit.

CREEPING POLEMONIUM (*Polemonium reptans*). Hardy, dwarf, upright creeper with bright blue flowers in April, May.

CREEPING SPEEDWELL (*Veronica repens*). Hardy, very low-growing (to 4 inches) deciduous trailer or creeper. Mosslike, with pink-blue flowers in May. Likes moist soil, shade.

CRIMSON MOSS (*Saxifraga decipiens*). Hardy deciduous ground cover with white flowers in May, June. Leaves turn bronze-crimson in fall.

DALMATION BELLFLOWER (*Campanula Portenschlagiana*). Hardy deciduous ground cover with blue-purple flowers in July. One of the most popular and colorful rock-garden plants. Likes sun.

DUSTY MILLER; BEACH WORMWOOD (*Artemisia Stelleriana*). Hardy, on the tall side as a ground cover but useful because of its ability to thrive in hot, dry, sandy conditions and to withstand salt-water spray. White, woolly, deeply-cut leaves; long spikes of small yellow flowers in summer.

GALAX (*Galax aphylla*). Hardy evergreen ground cover, with leaves turning a good red in fall. White flowers in July.

GROUND HEMLOCK (*Taxus canadensis*). Hardy evergreen trailer and ground cover, with unimportant flowers, bright red, berrylike fruit in August.

GROUND IVY (*Nepeta hederacea*). Hardy, deciduous, vigorous trailer and ground cover with minty-smelling leaves. Blue flowers May to September. Rapid low-grower in shade or sun—easily grows out of bounds if not controlled.

JAPANESE PACHYSANDRA (*Pachysandra terminalis*). One of the most satisfactory of the hardy ground covers growing even in deep shade of trees where nothing else will grow. Evergreen with white flowers in May, followed by white berries. Cannot stand full sun.

KENILWORTH IVY (*Cymbalaria muralis*). Semihardy deciduous ground cover with yellow-throated, lavender-blue flowers, May to October. Requires protection in the North. Likes moist soil, part shade.

LEMON THYME (*Thymus Serpyllum var. vulgaris*). Hardy evergreen trailer and ground cover with small lemon-scented leaves. Lavender to purple flowers in May, June.

MOROCCO CONVOLVULUS (*Convolvulus mauritanicus*). Hardy evergreen trailer often used in hanging baskets. Bears blue or purple flowers in July, August.

MOSS SANDWORT (*Arenaria verna caespitosa*). Hardiest, toughest and most rapid grower of the sandworts with mossy, evergreen leaves. Star-shaped, white flowers in May. Ideal for covering small bare spots of ground or planting between flagstones. Sun or shade.

MOUSE EAR GYPSOPHILA (*Gypsophila cerastioides*). Hardy, low-growing (to 4 inches), fast-spreading creeper with downy leaves. Covered with white, pink-veined flowers in May.

PARTRIDGE BERRY (*Mitchella repens*). Hardy evergreen trailer and ground cover with white flowers in May, followed by bright red fruit. Excellent for shady places. Likes woodsy and moist soil.

PEARLWORT (*Sagina subulata*). Very low-growing, mosslike evergreen ground cover, ideal for planting between cracks, steppingstones, etc. Bears small white flowers in July, August. Likes shade and is winter reliable to about southern Maine.

PURPLISH ARENARIA (*Arenaria purpurascens*). Hardy deciduous ground cover with rose-mauve flowers in May. The only Arenaria with colored flowers. Likes sun.

PUSSYTOES (*Antennaria dioica*). A hardy deciduous ground cover, of particularly good use in rock gardens. Bears white or rose flowers in June.

ROCKSPRAY (*Cotoneaster microphylla*). A very fine, semihardy, evergreen, small-leaved cotoneaster with white flowers in May, June, followed by red fruit. Likes sun, hardy to Massachusetts.

ROSY CREEPING GYPSOPHILA (*Gypsophila repens rosea*). One of the most notable hardy ground covers when in bloom. Bears rose flowers from late spring to midsummer. Likes sun and fairly dry alkaline soil.

RUNNING STRAWBERRY BUSH (*Euonymus obovatus*). Hardy deciduous trailer with uninteresting flowers, strawberry-colored fruit.

SAND LOVING PINK (*Dianthus arenarius*). Hardy evergreen ground cover and trailer with pleasantly fragrant, white flowers in June, July. Will stand shade but likes sun and sandy soil.

SARGENT JUNIPER (*Juniperus chinensis Sargentii*). Hardy, vigorous, evergreen, creeping shrub. Especially recommended for coastal areas. Forms a dense carpet often to 10 feet across. Blue berries in fall.

SHOWY SANDWORT (*Arenaria grandiflora*). A vigorous, hardy, deciduous trailer of rapid growth, with white flowers in June.

STONECROP (*Sedum var.*). Semihardy evergreen trailer and ground cover, widely popular in gardens for rock walls, etc. Bears white, yellow, rose flowers May to August. Usually survives Northern winters with protection.

SWAMP DEWBERRY (*Rubus hispidus*). Hardy, usually evergreen, very low-growing trailer and ground cover with many prickles. White, pink, or rose blossoms in June, July, followed by black fruit. Likes moist soil.

SWEET WOODRUFF (*Asperula odorata*). Hardy, especially vigorous ground cover which holds its own even in dense shade and in competition with greedy, shallow-rooted plants. Bears white flowers early May to mid-June.

THRIFT (*Armeria maritima*). Very hardy, low-growing evergreen, with foot-high stalks of white to deep-pink flowers in rounded heads, from late spring through early summer. Excellent for seashore conditions and the far North.

TURFING DAISY (*Matricaria Tchihatchewii*). Hardy, evergreen ground cover with white daisylike flowers June to August. Likes sun.

WEEPING FORSYTHIA (*Forsythia suspensa: see Forsythia under Rock Garden Plants and Shrubs, Trees, Hedges*). Hardy, deciduous, "weeping" type of **Golden Bells,** as it is often called. Blooms in April.

WHITLOWGRASS (*Draba vars.*). Hardy deciduous species of variable determination with white, yellow, or rose pink flowers in April, May, followed by small purplish pods.

WILLOW AMSONIA (*Amsonia Tabernaemontana*). Hardy deciduous ground cover, with exceptionally handsome green foliage until frost. Blue flowers May to July.

WILLOW HERB (*Epilobium nummularifolium*). Hardy ground cover with pink or whitish flowers in July. Likes moist soil.

WRINKLY MAZUS (*Mazus japonicus*). Handsome, hardy spreading ground cover forming low mat. Flowers are blue with lower lip spotted brown. Bloom June, July. Useful in rock gardens.

YELLOWNET JAPANESE HONEYSUCKLE (*Lonicera japonica var. aureo-reticulata*). Semihardy deciduous ground cover that grows in mounded clumps. White flowers June to September, followed by purple-black berries in fall. Hardy to Massachusetts.

Vines and Climbers

ARROWHEAD VINE (*Syngonium podophyllum vars.*). Tropical evergreen vine or creeper. Excellent for shady spots in hot humid climates. Climbs by means of aerial rootlets. Young plants have typical arrow-shaped leaves turning to 5 to 7 divided leaflets at maturity. Stands conditions of coastal areas. Some varieties have variegated leaves. Very sturdy and vigorous in rich moist soil. PROPAGATION: Cuttings.

1. ARROWHEAD VINE

BLACK-EYED SUSAN VINE (*Thunbergia alata*). Tender perennial vine grown as an annual in the North. Pretty, delicate flowers from yellow, orange, cream to pure white, some with typical purplish-black eye. Climbs by twining to about 5 feet and is ideal for covering low trellises, etc. Prefers semishade and rather light but rich soil. Start seeds outdoors as soon as possible; better yet, start them indoors in pots—they need long growing season. PROPAGATION: Seeds best in the North; cuttings (from side shoots).

2. BLACK-EYED SUSAN VINE

BOUGAINVILLEA (*Bougainvillea*). Tropical deciduous vine with climbing, slender, woody stems. Often pruned and used as a shrub (*see under Shrubs, Trees, Hedges*) in the far South. Very sturdy and vigorous, especially good for coastal regions as it stands up under wind and salt spray. Grown for its multitudinous cascades of flamboyant colored bracts in carmine, rose, white, rosy red, crimson, brick magenta. Leaves are small, ovate, green, in some varieties varie-

3. BOUGAINVILLEA

gated creamy white. Very tender, is harmed by temperature under 50 degrees if left for any length of time, but can stand full tropical sun; will also "bloom" with some light shade. PROPAGATION: Cuttings of half ripe wood.

CARDINAL CLIMBER (*Quamoclit Sloteri*). Tropical herbaceous vine often grown from seed as a summer-flowering vine. To 15 feet with dazzling crimson flowers, white throat; finely cut, glossy green leaves. A quick growing climber, covered with spectacular flowers from summer until frost. Easily trained to twine up string or wire or pole. Likes sun, and any good soil. PROPAGATION: Seed.

4. CARDINAL CLIMBER

CYPRESS VINE (*Quamoclit pennata*). Annual to 10 feet with long trumpet-shaped blossoms marked like a star in scarlet or pure white; very delicate, feathery green foliage. Quick growing, vigorous, a mass of blooms from summer until frost. Likes sun, average soil. PROPAGATION: Seed.

5. CYPRESS VINE

GLORY LILY (*Gloriosa*). Tender vine grown from tuberous root that climbs by means of leaf-tip tendrils. Superb flowers

6. GLORY LILY

with showy recurved petals in yellow and scarlet (*G. superba*); crimson and yellow (*G. Rothschildiana*). Will bloom in North first season; likes full sun but also blooms in light shade in any good soil. PROPAGATION: Offsets (in spring); seed (slow).

JAPANESE HONEYSUCKLE (*Lonicera japonica*). Hardy, vigorous, partially evergreen climber and ground cover; the most familiar honeysuckle in the eastern United

7. JAPANESE HONEYSUCKLE

States where it has "escaped" and become somewhat of a problem. Vigorous grower to 20 feet or more with woody twining stems; flowers white turning yellow, very fragrant. Other varieties have leaves variegated yellow (*aureo-reticulata*); or flowers red on outside, white inside (*chinensis*). The variety *Halliana* is very free blooming with typically white and yellow flowers and is evergreen. *Repens* has lower petals veined purple. Likes sun or shade; practically any soil. PROPAGATION: Hard to avoid as plant spreads rapidly by ground layering. Important to keep pruned within desired bounds (right after flowering).

MARBLE VINE (*Bryonopsis laciniosa*). An unusual and interesting annual vine, bearing glistening marblelike fruit that is yellow green with sharp white stripes when young, changing to amber and cream. It

8. MARBLE VINE

has good, substantial, deeply cut foliage (3 to 5 lobes). A good fast grower, excellent for shading a porch or a quick screening of a fence. Sun. PROPAGATION: Seed.

MEXICAN BREADFRUIT (*Monstera deliciosa*). Large, lush, vigorous tropical evergreen vine that attaches itself by means of aerial roots. Enormous deeply-notched leaves to 3 feet long. Often grown as a pot plant in the North and erroneously called

9. MEXICAN BREADFRUIT

cut-leaf philodendron. Excellent for shade or semishade; hot, humid climate (stands salty air of coastal areas). Likes any good soil. PROPAGATION: Cuttings.

MORNING GLORY (*Ipomoea purpurea*). Commonly known and listed as an annual but behaves like a tender perennial twining vine in tropical climates. Vigorous, fast-growing; blooms extensively over long periods (until frost). Ideal for quick covering wherever a vine is desired. Needs strong wires, stakes, trellis, fence, etc., to climb on. Flowers are large, showy, exquisitely colored such as the old favorite **Heavenly Blue** with large deep sky-blue flowers 4 to 5 inches across. **Blue Star** (4 to 5 inches) is pale or deep sky-blue with white midrib spears that form a showy star. (All-American Winner.) **Scarlet O'Hara** has brilliant rose red blooms 3½ inches across with scarlet "star" (All-American Gold

Medal Winner). **Pearly Gates** has the largest blooms (4½ inches) in snow white (All-American Silver Medal Winner). Morning glories easily climb from 8 to 12 feet or more, covered with a veritable sheet of blooms, but bloom only in the early morning or during cloudy or rainy days. Require full sun, any average soil. Seeds rather slow

10. MORNING GLORY (Heavenly Blue)

to germinate and you are usually advised to notch and soak them in warm water before planting, or to start seeds indoors in individual pots. PROPAGATION: Seeds.

PASSION FLOWER (*Passiflora alato-caerulea*). A tender perennial hybrid vine climbing by tendrils; intricate, very showy, fragrant flowers to 4 inches across in white with pink inside; purple, blue, and white

11. PASSION FLOWER

crown; abundant lustrous three-lobed leaves. Hardy only in southernmost United States. Plant in spring in sun, in well-drained loam kept moist during growing season. Flowers freely even when young. Prune promptly after blooming to eliminate weak shoots and keep within desired space. PROPAGATION: Best from cuttings (take in early spring); ground layering.

ROSE [**CLIMBERS**] (*Rosa: see under Shrubs, Trees, Hedges*). Many species and varieties sending up long, lithe canes or shoots, some to 15 feet of growth in one year and must be loosely tied to "climb." Bloom mostly in June and July, sometimes

12. ROSE (Coral Satin Climber)

again in late summer to early fall. Usually among the most successful of roses if properly trained and pruned. Plant in good average soil in sunny location (can stand a little shade), cutting back plant to about half its height. Fresh shoots will soon appear which must be staked and tied. These will produce roses the following year. From then on, only the removal of canes that have borne the season's flowers need be cut back, permitting new shoots to grow and produce next season's flowers. Usually hardy, but do better with winter protection, particularly in colder regions. PROPAGATION: Do not try it; it is best to buy reliable plants. **Coral Satin Climber,** shown here, has fragrant coral-pink flowers 4 inches across in clusters of 4 or 5. Grows to 6 to 7 feet, reblooms in later summer. **Blaze** is a brilliant crimson, blooms June to September; myriad 2- to 3-inch flowers in clusters.

SWEET PEAS (*Lathyrus odoratus*). Annual vine climbing by means of tendrils. A great favorite for its lovely flowers, variety of colors and delicious fragrance. Many superb new strains such as the new **Galaxy® Gigi** shown here—a light salmon-cerise; also pink, blue, lavender, white, cerise, flame, rose in many tones. Likes cool weather and makes fastest growth in early spring. Rich well-drained soil, sun, plenty of moisture at all times; fall sowing often preferable in mild climates. PROPAGATION: Seed.

13. SWEET PEA (Gigi)

VIRGINIA CREEPER; WOODBINE (*Parthenocissus quinquefolia*). Hardy, perennial, deciduous vine; exceedingly vigorous and fast growing in sun or shade. Also used as creeper or ground cover. Very useful for shady walls or fences; leaves turn bright red in fall. Climbs by tendrils that attach themselves with suckerlike force to anything that is around. Like rich woodsy moist soil but will even grow on sand dunes in coastal areas. Must be pruned vigorously to keep within bounds. PROPAGATION: Plant naturally ground-layers itself, can easily be cut from the parent and transplanted. Keep moist and shaded until established.

14. VIRGINIA CREEPER

WINTER CREEPER (*Euonymus Fortunei radicans*). Hardy evergreen perennial vine climbing by rootlets that grow from its stems. Many excellent varieties with glossy leaves of excellent substance, some margined in yellow, white, or pink; others turning purplish red from fall till spring. Often used as a creeper for ground cover or in rock gardens. Likes sunny to half-shady location, any good soil. PROPAGATION: Easy from cuttings in spring; division.

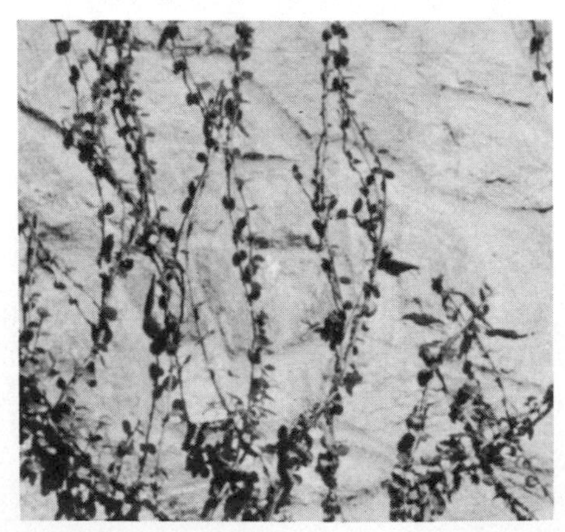

15. WINTER CREEPER

WISTERIA (*Wisteria*). Deciduous, perennial, woody twining vines with long drooping racemes of unusually fragrant, lovely flowers. Very rapid and vigorous grower, apt to go out of bounds, ripping out everything in its path (including rain spouts, etc.) if not kept properly pruned. Excellent for covering entire walls of buildings, high fences, etc. The two favorite species are: **Chinese Wisteria** (*W. Chinensis*)—racemes to about 1 foot long with 1-inch-long flowers in mauve, white (*alba*); blue (*caerulea*), violet-purple (*purpurea*). **Japanese Wisteria** (*W. floribunda*)—racemes to 1½ feet long in violet blue; white (*alba*); flesh tone (*carnea*). In the Japanese variety *longissima* or *macrobotys*, racemes reach a length of 3 to 4 feet in pale pink, rose-red, reddish, lavender, some double. Both species hardy in the North. CULTURE: Wisteria does best in sunny location against a southwest or south wall; any average soil (actually too rich a soil produces more foliage than blooms). Failure to produce blooms is usually due to improper pruning (it is assumed you are buying grafted stock, not seedlings which will not bloom for years). Flowers are produced from spurlike growths numerous on side shoots. Once the plant has covered the desired area allocated to it, systematically pinch back side growth to the seventh leaf all during the summer. Then, in winter, ruthlessly prune these

16. WISTERIA

back to within 3 inches of their bases. Another way to encourage blooming is to prune the roots as well as the shoots. PROPAGATION: Best is ground layering of lower branches; root cuttings.

More Vines and Climbers

AMERICAN BITTERSWEET (*Celastrus scandens*). Hardy, twining, climbing shrub with orange-yellow fruit in June. Half shade.

AMERICAN CLIMBING HYDRANGEA (*Decumaria barbara*). Deciduous, with white flowers in May, June. Good for walls, rocks, and trellises. Hardy to Massachusetts. Sun.

BALLOON VINE (*Cardiospermum Halicacabum*). Annual (sometimes biennial or perennial in warm climates). White flowers July to October. Attractive, balloonlike fruit. Sun.

BOSTON IVY (*Parthenocissus tricuspidata*). Excellent climber on walls, trees, or unsightly rock piles. Bears greenish flower in July; black, berrylike fruit. Hardy to Massachusetts. Sun or part shade.

BOWER ACTINIDIA (*Actinidia arguta*). Makes marvelous fence if supported. Has white flower in July, greenish-yellow fruit. Deciduous. Hardy to Massachusetts. Sun or part shade.

CALICO FLOWER (*Aristolochia elegans*). Tender, deciduous, handsome, large-leaved; often grown as porch vine. Flowers in July, purplish-brown inside, white, veined-purple outside. Part shade.

CANARY BIRD (*Tropaeolum peregrinum*). Annual with yellow, green-spurred flowers in July, August. Sun.

CHILEAN GLORYFLOWER (*Eccremocarpus scaber*). Annual in the North, perennial in the South. Bright, orange-red flowers September, October. Sun or light shade.

CHINESE MATRIMONY VINE; BOXTHORN; TEA TREE (*Lycium chinense*). Hardy deciduous climber, with purple flowers May to September, followed by orange-red to scarlet berries. Good for coastal areas. Sun.

CHINESE SILKVINE (*Periploca sepium*). Deciduous, with greenish flowers, brownish-purple inside, July to September. Hardy to Massachusetts. Sun.

CHINESE TRUMPET CREEPER (*Campsis chinensis*). Semihardy climber with scarlet flowers July, August. Requires winter protection in the North. Sun.

CLIMBING FUMITORY (*Adlumia fungosa*). A most graceful, semihardy, biennial climber with white or purplish flower in July, August. Requires winter protection in the North. Shade.

CLIMBING HYDRANGEA (*Hydrangea petiolaris*). Handsome deciduous climber with white flower June, July. Requires winter protection in the far North. Sun.

ENGELMANN CREEPER (*Parthenocissus quinquefolia var. Engelmanii*). Hardy, deciduous. Makes excellent screen for brick, stone, or other solid surfaces. Flowers: greenish in July, August, followed by black berry. Sun or semishade.

ENGLISH IVY (*Hedera Helix*). Splendid, hardy, evergreen climber or ground cover with greenish flower in September, October, followed by black fruit. Does better with winter protection in North. Sun or semishade.

FIVE-LEAF AKEBIA (*Akebia quinata*). Hardy, half-evergreen to January, with purplish flower in May followed by purple berry. Sun.

GROUNDNUT (*Apios tuberosa*). Hardy, deciduous, with wisterialike foliage. Brown fragrant flowers July, August. Likes moist soil. Sun, light shade.

HALL JAPANESE HONEYSUCKLE (*Lonicera japonica var. Halliana*). Excellent hardy evergreen honeysuckle for covering banks or trellises, etc. White flowers changing to yellow, June to September, followed by black fruit. Sun or light shade.

HOP (*Humulus Lupulus*). Hardy, deciduous. An excellent vine for covering walls, fences, trellises, etc. Bears chartreuse flowers July, August. Sun.

HYACINTH BEAN (*Dolichos Lablab*). Semihardy perennial often grown as an annual with purple, white flower June to August. Requires winter protection in North if wanted to carry over. Sun.

ITALIAN JASMINE (*Jasminum humile*). Evergreen with very fragrant yellow flowers July to September. Hardy to Washington, D.C. Sun or light shade.

JACKMAN CLEMATIS (*Clematis Jackmanii*). Hardy herbaceous vine, with violet-purple flower July, August. Sun.

JAPANESE HOP (*Humulus japonicus*). Fast-growing annual climber, well suited to porches or screens. Small retiring flowers July, August. Sun.

JAPANESE HYDRANGEA VINE (*Schizophragma hydrangeoides*). Deciduous, semihardy, herbaceous vine, with white flowers in July. Hardy to Philadelphia. Sun or semishade.

KUDZU VINE (*Pueraria Thunbergiana*). Fast-growing perennial vine with purple flowers in August. Hardy to Philadelphia. Sun.

LALAND FIRETHORN (*Pyracantha coccinea var. Lalandi*). Arresting, colorful, with white flowers in May, followed by brilliant orange-red fruit. Hardy. Sun.

MADEIRA VINE (*Boussingaultia baselloides*). Perennial. Rapid cover for banks, rock piles, etc. White flowers July to September. Best with winter protection in North. Sun.

MATRIMONY VINE (*Lycium halimifolium*). Hardy deciduous climber, good for walls. Lilac-purple flower May to September, followed by orange-red berries. Sun.

MONKSHOOD VINES (*Ampelopsis aconitifolia*). Hardy, deciduous, with greenish flower in July, followed by yellow-orange fruit. Sun or light shade.

MOON FLOWER (*Calonyction aculeatum*). Tender night-blooming perennial grown as annual in the North. Bears white flowers, often banded green, July to October. Sun.

MOONSEED (*Menispermum canadense*). Hardy, deciduous, with small white or pale yellow flowers in June, July, followed by black fruit. Sun or light shade.

NASTURTIUM (*Tropaeolum majus*). Annual with masses of yellow or orange flowers marked red or chocolate, July, August. Sun.

ORIENTAL BITTERSWEET (*Celastrus articulatus*). Hardy, highly ornamental, with yellow fruit, orange seed. Sun or light shade.

ORIENTAL CLEMATIS (*Clematis orientalis*). Hardy, deciduous, good for low trellises, fences, etc. Yellow flowers in August, September. Sun.

PERENNIAL PEA (*Lathyrus latifolius*). Hardy, deciduous with sweet-pea-type rose flowers July to September. Semishade or shade.

PIEDMONT BUTTERFLY PEA (*Centrosema virginianum*). Hardy, evergreen, twining vine with purple to whitish flower in August, pods to 5 inches long. Sun.

PORCELAIN AMPELOPSIS (*Ampelopsis brevipedunculata var. Maximowiczii*). Hardy, deciduous, attractive vine, popular for porches, etc. Greenish flowers in July, followed by lilac to blue fruit. Sun, light shade.

PURPLEBELL COBAEA (*Cobaea scandens*). Annual with violet, greenish-purple flower in July, August. Moist soil. Sun.

RIVERBANK GRAPE (*Vitis vulpina*). Hardy, deciduous, vigorous climber with dull black fruit. Sun or light shade.

SILVER LACE VINE; CHINA FLEECE VINE (*Polygonum Aubertii*). Hardy herbaceous perennial with greenish-white flowers June to September. Sun or light shade.

SILVER VINE (*Actinidia polygama*). Deciduous, popular for terrace or porch. Bears white flower in July, followed by yellow fruit. Hardy to Massachusetts. Sun or light shade.

SQUIRTING CUCUMBER (*Ecballium Elaterium*). Perennial grown as annual, with yellow flower in June, followed by fruit seeds which can be made to squirt. Requires winter protection in North if treated as perennial. Sun.

SUAKWA TOWEL GOURD (*Luffa cylindrica*). Annual with yellow, white flower in July, followed by green fruit. Sun.

SUMMER GRAPE (*Vitis aestivalis*). Tender to semihardy, vigorous, very tall and fast-growing vine with large leaves; blooms May, June. Black fruit. For mild climates but can be grown in central states with protection. Sun.

SWEET AUTUMN CLEMATIS (*Clematis paniculata*). Hardy, herbaceous, tall climber, with white flowers in September, October. Sun.

THREE-LEAF AKEBIA (*Akebia trifoliata*). Semihardy, half evergreen, with purplish flowers in May, followed by attractive purple fruit. Should have winter protection in North. Sun or light shade.

TRICOLOR MORNING GLORY (*Ipomoea tricolor vars.*). Tender perennial grown as annual in the North. Masses of highly colorful purple, blue, pink tricolored flowers July, August. Sun.

TRUMPET HONEYSUCKLE (*Lonicera sempervirens*). Hardy evergreen with orange-scarlet flower, yellow inside, May to August, followed by red fruit. Sun or light shade.

TRUMPET VINE (*Campsis radicans*). Deciduous, highly ornamental, with orange-crimson flowers in July, August. Hardy to Massachusetts. Sun.

WILD PASSION FLOWER (*Passiflora incarnata*). White flower, crowned purple, pink, in July, August, followed by yellow fruit. Hardy to Virginia. Sun or light shade.

WILD SWEET POTATO VINE (*Ipomoea pandurata*). Hardy vigorous perennial, apt to get out of bounds unless controlled. Bears purple-throated white flowers in July, August. Sun.

WIND CUCUMBER (*Echinocystis lobata*).Vigorous annual climber with white, greenish flowers, followed by spiny crimson fruit July to October. Sun.

WINTER JASMINE (*Jasminum nudiflorum*). Deciduous, reliably hardy to Washington, D.C. Pretty yellow flowers in April, May. Sun or light shade.

Shrubs, Trees, Hedges

APPLE (*Malus*). Hardy, deciduous trees or shrubs, mostly grown for their fruit although some of the crab apples may be chiefly raised as ornamentals. Bloom in spring with masses of pink-white flowers. The popular decorative small trees belong to the **Showy Crab Apple** (*M. floribunda*)

1. SHOWY CRAB APPLE

group with lovely deep rose blossoms and an abundance of red, eminently preservable fruit. Dwarfs seem to bear well and are ideally suited for small spaces.

ARALIA (*Polyscias Balfouriana*). Tender evergreen trees and shrubs to 25 feet with highly ornamental foliage, green, or green strongly marked with white. Widely planted in warm climates, particularly coastal areas since they seem to stand wind and salt spray. Often used as decorative privacy hedge for terraces.

2. ARALIA

ARBOR VITAE; WOODWARD'S GLOBE (*Thuja occidentalis Woodwardii*). Hardy, evergreen tree. Dense and globular

3. ARBOR VITAE

with frondlike branches, tiny, scaly, deep-green leaves. Prized for its dwarf, slow, compact, symmetrical growth. Makes excellent, low, dense hedge although subject to winter burn. Stands shearing well.

AUSTRALIAN PINE (*Casuarina*). Tender evergreen trees and shrubs with graceful feathery foliage. Favorite avenue trees of seacoast regions, well suited to salt-water spray, alkaline soils, to hold sands, etc. Often planted as hedges and windbreaks in mild climates.

4. AUSTRALIAN PINE

AUSTRIAN PINE (*Pinus nigra*). Hardy, evergreen, commanding, dense tree; vigorous under adverse conditions such as strong winds, salt spray, lime soils, etc. An excellent shelter tree with stiff dark-green leaves to 6½ inches long at maturity; oval cones 3½ inches long. Marvelous, thick, tall windbreak when planted as a hedge.

5. AUSTRIAN PINE

AZALEA (*Rhododendron*). All azaleas are Rhododendron to the botanists but we generally refer to azaleas as deciduous shrubs and to Rhododendron as evergreen shrubs with large, deep-green, leathery leaves. Whatever their name azaleas are among the most brilliant of flowering shrubs in a wide range of color from white, pale yellow, apricot, pink, orchid, orange, salmon, magenta red, depending on the type. It is best to consult the local nursery for the proper species for your area, as many of the hardy types will not grow in warm climates and the tender kinds are suited only as potted subjects in the North. All like partial shade and any soil that is not alkaline. Working peat moss into the soil is a good safeguard.

6. AZALEA

BALSAM FIR (*Abies balsamea*). Hardy evergreen used extensively as a Christmas tree. Tall, symmetrical, pyramidal shape, excellent for moist, well-drained soil and moist climates but not for wind-swept locations. Flat linear leaves about 1 inch long. Erect oblong cones (2½ inches long) with deciduous scales. There are also dwarf forms.

7. BALSAM FIR

BLACK WALNUT (*Juglans nigra*). Fast growing, long-lived, very hardy, deciduous ornamental tree that bears large crops of

8. BLACK WALNUT

excellent black walnuts annually. Grows almost anywhere in the country. To 40 feet.

BOUGAINVILLEA (*Bougainvillea: see under Vines and Climbers*). Since Bougainvillea is so widely grown in warm climates as a shrub or hedge, it is shown here again to give you some idea of its silhouette. What you see are not leaves but a mass of explosive scarlet bracts growing in the white coral sands of the Florida Keys.

9. BOUGAINVILLEA

BRIDAL WREATH (*Spiraea prunifolia*). Deciduous, hardy, one of the most attrac-

10. BRIDAL WREATH

tive of spring-flowering shrubs, densely covered with graceful clusters of tiny pure white flowers. To about 6 feet. Easy to grow in any good soil in sunny location. Stands seacoast conditions well.

CAMELLIA (*Camellia*). Favorite evergreen flowering trees and shrubs of the South and Pacific coast and possibly soon of

11. CAMELLIA

colder climates since Camellias are now developed that are reputed to withstand freezing. Glossy, dark-green leaves, superb flowers, single, semidouble, and double in white, pink, rose, red, and variegated, produced in masses generally from fall to spring, but mine (which live in pots indoors in winter), upon being moved outdoors in spring, immediately produce more buds and bloom well into early September. Of simple culture in rather rich peaty (acid) soil; like plenty of moisture, humidity, part shade.

CHINESE CHESTNUT (*Castanea mollissima*). Hardy, deciduous, useful as shade tree as well as a source of delicious, large nuts. Grows 30 to 60 feet. Blight-resistant. Plant two or more in close proximity for nuts.

12. CHINESE CHESTNUT

COLORADO BLUE SPRUCE (*Picea pungens glauca*). Hardy, evergreen, tall

13. COLORADO BLUE SPRUCE

pyramidal tree with radial-spreading, spiny, blue leaves. Among the most beautiful of the spruces. Has long drooping cones with persistent scales to 4 inches long. Many excellent varieties with silvery white, green, blue-green foliage. Some dwarfs, some with drooping branches.

DOGWOOD (*Cornus florida*). Hardy, deciduous, one of the most decorative of the

14. DOGWOOD

small trees (15 to 35 feet) with large white or pink to rose bracts in profusion in spring. Small bright red fruit and brilliant leaves in fall.

DOUGLAS FIR (*Pseudotsuga taxifolia, P. Douglasii*). Hardy evergreen of magnificent stature, a fine cone-bearing tree and a fa-

15. DOUGLAS FIR

vorite for Christmas. Pyramidal and compact when young, opening to show reddish bark at maturity. Soft bluish-green leaves, resembling fir leaves in shape (as close-up shows here). 4½-inch drooping cones have deciduous scales. Easily transplanted, likes rather light soil.

EUROPEAN BEECH (*Fagus sylvatica*). Hardy, deciduous, an outstanding ornamental tree with tall stately branches, sometimes drooping to the ground and rooting. Many varieties with beautiful colored foliage, purplish, copper, rose bordered; some margined, some tricolor. To 90 feet. Also a superb hedge since it remains leafy and dense even when clipped.

16. EUROPEAN BEECH

FORSYTHIA (*Forsythia*). Hardy, deciduous, favorite flowering shrub, one of the earliest spring bloomers with golden-yellow flowers borne in profusion often before the leaves appear. Many new forms now developed in different heights with flowers of exceptionally large sizes, including the "tree" form, shown here. A showy ornamental shrub by itself or highly colorful hedge (see photo). Easy to grow in any soil, stands seacoast conditions well.

17. TREE FORSYTHIA (Stern's)

FUCHSIA (*Fuchsia*). Tender evergreen plants (1½ to 20 feet, depending on the species). Grown widely on the Pacific coast as ornamental shrubs, colorful hedges trained as climbers or to "tree" form. In the North they are grown as summer bedders, pot plants, in hanging baskets. Modern hybrids are superb in color and shade. Graceful flowers in drooping terminal clusters in single colors or in combinations of pink, magenta, white, lavender. They like part shade.

18. FUCHSIA (Pride of Orion)

GARDENIA (*Gardenia*). Tender evergreen flowering shrub or small tree with shining oval green leaves and masses of fragrant white waxy blooms, single or double. They like sun and somewhat acid soil with plenty of peat, high atmospheric humidity. A highly prized shrub for mild climates, grown as a pot plant in the North.

19. GARDENIA

GRAY BIRCH; WHITE BIRCH (*Betula populifolia*). Hardy, deciduous, one of the most attractive ornamental trees summer

20. GRAY BIRCH

or winter because of its glistening white bark (at maturity); of clumping habit. The **Paper-** or **Canoebirch** (*B. papyrifera*) has white, shaggy, parchmentlike bark; the **European White Birch** (*B. pendula*) has white bark that peels off in layers. All relatively short-lived.

HELIOTROPE (*Heliotropium arborescens*). Tender shrubs (to 6 feet) often used

21. HELIOTROPE

as summer bedding pot plants or hanging baskets in the North. They have typically hairy green leaves and tiny, delicate, lavender-blue fragrant flowers in terminal clusters. Like sun, fairly rich peaty soil.

HIBISCUS (*Hibiscus*). Tender and hardy shrubs from 8 to 10 feet with large showy flowers. Tender kinds are grown chiefly in Southern Florida and Southern California as they can stand practically no frost. Flowers up to 5 inches across, single or double, in brilliant salmon, coral, pink, apricot, yellow, white and scarlet. Often planted as a decorative hedge; stand shearing well. Tolerate to full sun and seashore conditions. Hardy Hibiscus are often called **Althea** or **Rose of Sharon.** These are deciduous shrubs with single or double flowers, in lavender, pale blue, bluish, white, rose, red. Bloom best in sun.

22. HIBISCUS

HICKORY (*Carya*). Hardy, deciduous, tall (80 to 150 feet) trees prized for their

23. HICKORY

nuts, particularly the **Pecan** (*Carya Pecan*) much grown in the South. Grown in the Northeast as a shade tree (nuts will not ripen there). A valuable tree, with handsome bark and colorful yellow leaves in fall. Not easily transplanted.

HONEY LOCUST (*Gleditsia triacanthos inermis*). Hardy, deciduous, to 140 feet. Vigorous, fast-growing, very beautiful shade tree noted for its lacy foliage and its ability to attract bees. Has small fragrant greenish blossoms in early summer, followed by long, glossy, brown beanlike pods that grow to 1½ feet long and that last until winter. Unlike most Honey Locusts this variety has no thorns.

24. HONEY LOCUST

JAPANESE ANDROMEDA (*Pieris japonica*). Hardy, evergreen shrub with substan-

25. JAPANESE ANDROMEDA

tial, broad, light-green leaves in fall, rich bronze in spring. Bears masses of creamy white flowers in long 5-inch pendulous clusters. Likes somewhat acid, moist soil; shade or sun.

JUNIPER (Hetz Blue) (*Juniperus chinensis Pfizeriana Hetzii glauca*). Hardy evergreen tree of irregular, spreading, prostate habit without central leader. Attractive broad-spreading, much branched scaly bluish leaves. A fast grower in the sun.

26. JUNIPER (Hetz Blue)

LANTANA (*Lantana*). Tender evergreen shrubs 2 to 6 feet with large clusters of tiny flowers in pink, lavender, cream, yellow,

27. LANTANA

orange, scarlet, often several colors on one cluster. Used for planting outdoors in mild climates. Dwarf hybrids often used as summer bedding plants in the North. Like sun.

LILAC (*Syringa*). Hardy, deciduous shrubs (to 20 feet) with large fragrant clusters of

28. LILAC

lavender, blue, red-purple, purple white or cream flowers, single or double. Probably the most popular single shrub of temperate climates. Needs sun and rich loam for good blooms and should be kept vigorous by removal of suckers and weak shoots. Pruning should be on the conservative side and consist of little more than removing old growth from the base. Flowers form on new wood. Makes handsome, tall, informal hedges.

LOMBARDY POPLAR (*Populus nigra italica*). Hardy, deciduous, tall (to 80 feet) tree often planted 2 to 3 feet apart and used

29. LOMBARDY POPLAR

for a windbreak or as a screen. Fast growing, naturally graceful, requires no pruning to maintain its columnar shape.

MAGNOLIA (*Magnolia Soulangeana*). Hardy, deciduous, small hybrid trees with a profusion of large, handsome flowers in

30. MAGNOLIA

spring. There are several varieties, generally blooming from spring through early summer with flowers mainly white or white-suffused-purple to rosy-purple. Like a peaty, acid soil.

MALPIGHIA (*Malpighia coccigera*). Tender, highly ornamental shrub to 3 feet, widely grown in warm climates for its attractive shape, tiny hollylike leaves and its profusion of delicate pink flowers followed by bright red fruit. Easy to grow in any good soil; stands hot sun, seacoast conditions well. Often grown as pot plant in the North.

31. MALPIGHIA

MOCK ORANGE (*Philadelphus coronarius*). Hardy, deciduous shrubs with very fragrant, orange-blossom scented, white blooms in spring. Each flower about 1¼ inches across, single or double, usually in clusters of from 5 to 10. Spreading and shrubby, almost as wide as it is high (12 to 15 feet). There are many varieties, some with golden leaves, some variegated; some dwarf, some tall.

32. MOCK ORANGE

MORAINE LOCUST (*Gleditsia triacanthos var.: trade-marked plant patent 1313*). Hardy deciduous tree with feathery foliage so fine it all but vanishes after falling. Rapidly challenging the American Elm for its popularity as a shade tree . . . shaped much like the Elm but disease-resistant. Unlike its relatives the Honey Locusts, this variety does not produce seeds or thorns. A handsome shapely tree, vigorous, fast-growing even in the city.

33. MORAINE LOCUST

NORWAY MAPLE (*Acer platanoides*). Hardy, deciduous, excellent shade and ornamental tree, many with highly colored and decorative leaves. From 50 to 100 feet depending on the variety. Leaves light or dark green; margined or spotted white or yellow, greenish red to red, bright red, purple.

34. NORWAY MAPLE

NORWAY SPRUCE (*Picea Abies, P. excelsa*). Hardy, evergreen, fast-growing tree. One of the best, if not the prettiest, spruces known. Useful for moist situations, as a hedge or windbreak. Very hardy, grows to 200 feet under ideal situations in Europe, usually smaller here. Many varieties with variable habits, length and color of leaves (usually dark green and shiny).

35. NORWAY SPRUCE

OLEANDER (*Nerium Oleander*). Tender evergreen shrub or small tree to 20 feet. An old-fashioned favorite of the South and mild climate coastal regions for its profusion of handsome flowers—single, semi-double, and double in glistening white, pink, rose, red, apricot. Ideal for hot, sandy conditions; often planted as a tall unclipped hedge or windbreak.

36. OLEANDER

ORCHID TREE (*Bauhinia*). Tender evergreen trees and shrubs from 15 to 30 feet

37. ORCHID TREE

high, with large, sometimes fragrant, very beautiful flowers—pink marked purple, or white through lavender to purple—followed by long decorative pods. Stand full sun and coastal conditions well.

PIN OAK (*Quercus palustris*). Hardy, deciduous tree to 80 feet tall. Pyramid shaped of excellent symmetry. Deeply cut foliage turns scarlet in fall. A rapid grower; one of the best shade trees.

38. PIN OAK

PRIVET; PRIM (*Ligustrum vulgare*). The hardiest and toughest of the privets, probably the most widely used for hedges, windbreaks. Able to stand almost any climate, any soil, sun, or part shade. Deciduous, not quite as handsome as **California Privet** (*L. ovalifolium*), but more reliable in cold areas. Good for city and coastal areas, stands shearing well, can even be used to hold shifting sands. Grows to 15 feet or so and bears clusters of white scented flowers if left untrimmed.

39. PRIVET

RED OAK; SCARLET OAK (*Quercus coccinea*). Hardy, deciduous, to 80 feet. One of the handsomest oaks with leaves turning brilliant scarlet in fall. Fast growing, easy to transplant even at an advanced age. Of good upright form—a favorite shade tree.

40. RED OAK

RED PINE (*Pinus resinosa*). Hardy, evergreen, fast-growing tree also known as the **Norway Pine.** Of dense conical shape, it is excellent used as an ornamental or as a hedge or windbreak. One of the hardiest evergreens, growing to 100 feet. Glossy leaves in clusters to 6 inches long at maturity. Oval-conical cones to 2½ inches long.

41. RED PINE

RHODODENDRON HYBRIDS (*Rhododendron*). Popular, important evergreen shrubs with massive clusters of flowers ranging from reds and scarlets to mauves

42. RHODODENDRON HYBRIDS

and white. Although the hybrids are generally hardier and better able to withstand a little more dryness and cold, in general Rhododendrons do best in the Pacific Northwest and along the eastern seaboard. The far North is too cold for them, the South too hot, and the central plains too dry in summer, too cold in winter. Blooming season has been extended, too, and in a favorable location they may bloom from early spring into summer. Require woodsy peaty soil, kept moist but not soggy, and generally do best sheltered from strong winds. Plant reds and scarlets in part shade, mauves and whites in heavier shade.

ROSE (*Rosa: see also under Vines*). Mostly hardy, deciduous, probably the most popular of all flowering shrubs. Excellent for beginners since modern types are almost foolproof in any halfway decent soil, bloom

43. ROSE (Hybrid Tea Nobility)

lavishly and often for long periods with relatively little care. Colors, fragrance and form are unsurpassed. Here is a brief description of the most common classifications. *Hybrid Teas* are compact, shrubby plants with single, large blooms on a stem, such as **Hybrid Tea Nobility,** shown here, a fresh pastel pink with blooms 5 to 5½ inches in diameter. *Floribunda* is the generic name for roses that bloom in clusters such as **Girl Scout,** shown here, with rich golden blossoms 3½ inches in diameter borne 3 or more on a stem. They are often planted as borders or low hedges, as **Golden**

Fleece, shown here. In this classification are included the *Hybrid Polyanthas*. *Grandiflora* roses are a cross between *Floribunda* and *Hybrid Teas* producing the best

44. ROSE (Girl Scout)

characteristics of each—fewer but larger blooms to a cluster. *Hybrid Perpetuals* are

45. ROSE (Golden Fleece)

the grandparents of *Hybrid Teas*. These are very vigorous with large fragrant flowers of a less formal shape than *Hybrid Teas*, such as **Stern's Queen of the Violets,** shown here. *Pillar, Fountain* and *Tree Roses* are really not a different classification but a shrub-type rose grafted to a tall sturdy single strong stem rose, usually a *Brier* or *Rugosa*. By this method one can get tricky combinations such as **Stern's Rainbow** four-in-one tree rose with four different blooms

46. ROSE (Stern's Queen of the Violets)

on one "tree." These generally are not reputed to be as reliable as bush-type roses. There are of course dozens of other types of roses—dwarfs, miniatures, etc.— all in the typical range of colors—white, ivory, pinks, yellow, golds, coral, rose, red, copper, bronze, garnet and the new range of lavenders and orange. CULTURE: Given any reasonably sunny location and good well-drained soil, roses will generally do well. Since there seems to be such a variety of instructions on how and when to fertilize and prune, etc., I guess my system is as good as any. Pruning consists of nothing more than tidying up and general housekeeping. That is, I cut back all dead wood to live tissue in the spring, old dead canes to the ground and remove all weak twiggy growth. During the growing season I keep spent blossoms plucked off, give plants an occasional light shaping to keep the rare straggly growth under control, and remove diseased tissue as promptly as I can get to it. I try to fertilize at least once a year, but if I forget, I get masses of roses anyway. Although winter protection is usually recommended I have never done it and all seem to survive freezing and thawing, heavy snows, even the regular flood conditions I live in. In far northern regions they probably would be less apt to survive without cover.

SCOTCH PINE (*Pinus sylvestris*). Hardy evergreen tree, one of the hardiest pines.

47. SCOTCH PINE

Dense bluish-green leaves, 2 in a sheath, 2 to 3 inches long, oval cones 2½ inches long. Relatively short lived, some 40 years being about par for the course. Many types developed some with orange bark, short branches; some with golden leaves or silver variegated branches; some low and globular, some slender and erect, some dwarfs. Excellent as a hedge and windbreak.

STAR MAGNOLIA (*Magnolia stellata*). Hardy, deciduous, shapely . . . one of the first shrubs to bloom in spring, its leafless branches covered with large glistening starlike white flowers. Likes peaty soil, sun

48. STAR MAGNOLIA

or light shade. Stands seacoast conditions well; grows 10 to 15 feet.

SUGAR MAPLE (*Acer saccharum*). Hardy, deciduous, to 120 feet. This is *the* maple of maple products, one of the most prized trees. Also a superb shade tree with leaves turning a flamboyant yellow-orange-scarlet in the fall.

49. SUGAR MAPLE

TULIP TREE; TULIP POPLAR (*Liriodendron Tulipifera*). Hardy, deciduous,

50. TULIP TREE

handsomely symmetrical tree with glossy fiddle-shaped leaves. Decorative chartreuse and orange tuliplike flowers. One of the largest, most remarkable of ornamental and timber trees. Grows to 200 feet.

WEEPING WILLOW, WISCONSIN (*Salix blanda*). Hardy, deciduous, hybrid tree with either golden or green bark, long gracefully arched weeping branches with pendulous, fluttering leaves. Extremely rapid grower (to 30 feet) if given plenty of water (so strong it will grow right through your plumbing system too!). Excellent near pools or streams; will stand salt spray. Cut back branchlets frequently to induce thicker growth.

51. WISCONSIN WEEPING WILLOW

WEST INDIAN JASMINE; IXORA (*Ixora*). Tender evergreen flowering shrub

52. WEST INDIAN JASMINE

to 4 feet with large clusters of white, rose, or scarlet flowers, highly ornamental foliage. An excellent shrub for mild climates, stands sun and seacoast conditions well.

WHITE PINE (*Pinus Strobus*). Hardy evergreen tree, one of the most magnificent tall coniferous pines growing to 150 feet.

53. WHITE PINE

Thick clusters of soft, blue-green leaves, 5 in a sheath, to 5 inches long. Cylinder-shaped cones to 4 inches. There are many varieties . . . some with golden leaves, some dwarf, bushy or trailing forms. Good as hedge and windbreak.

YEW, HICK'S (*Taxus media Hicksii*). Hardy evergreen, bushy tree with many erect, ascending branches. Makes excellent dense, evergreen hedge (2 to 5 feet) or handsome solitary tree. Leaves are a bright dark green.

54. HICK'S YEW

More Shrubs

ADAM LABURNUM (*Laburnocytisus Adamii*). From 10 to 30 feet. Hardy, deciduous. Interesting graft hybrid. Some branches with flowers yellow suffused with purple, some with purple-pink; some with yellow. Blooms May, June.

ALBANIAN FORSYTHIA (*Forsythia europaea*). To 6 feet. Very hardy, deciduous; yellow flowers appear in April before foliage.

ALMOND TREE (*Prunus communis*). To 25 feet. Hardy, deciduous. A double-flowering almond with pink flowers in May followed by inedible oblong fruit.

AMERICAN ELDERBERRY (*Sambucus canadensis*). To 12 feet. Hardy, deciduous.

White flowers in June, July followed by edible purple-black fruit.

AMERICAN HOLLY (*Ilex opaca*). To 50 feet. Hardy, evergreen. White flowers in June followed by dull red berries, sometimes yellow.

AMERICAN JAMESIA (*Jamesia americana*). To 3 feet. Hardy, deciduous, with white flowers in May, June. Foliage turns orange and scarlet in autumn.

AUSTRALIAN BRUSH CHERRY (*Eugenia paniculata var. australis*). To 12 feet. Tender evergreen. Flowers white or whitish in April, May followed by rose-purple edible berries. Warm climates only.

BAILEY DOGWOOD (*Cornus Baileyi*). To 10 feet. Hardy, deciduous, with reddish branches, white flowers in May, followed by white fruit. Recommended for sandy soil.

BALKAN DAPHNE (*Daphne Blagayana*). To 1 foot. Hardy, evergreen, with small cream, sweet-scented flowers in April.

BAYBERRY (*Myrica caroliniensis*). To 9 feet. Hardy, deciduous to evergreen, with grayish-white fruit in June.

BEAUTY BUSH (*Kolkwitzia amabilis*). To 6 feet. Hardy, deciduous; very graceful with pink, yellow-throated flowers in May, June.

BLACK ALDER (*Ilex verticillata*). To 10 feet. Semihardy, deciduous. Whitish flowers in June, July followed by bright red berries. Protect in North.

BLADDER SENNA (*Colutea arborescens*). To 15 feet. Hardy, deciduous, with yellow flowers June to September, followed by bronze-red fruit.

BLOODTWIG DOGWOOD (*Cornus sanguinea*). To 12 feet. Hardy, deciduous, with greenish-white flowers in May, June. Fruit black; purple or red branches.

BLUEBEARD (*Caryopteris incana*). To 5 feet. Semihardy, deciduous, flowers violet or lavender-blue August to November. Protect in North.

BOG ROSEMARY (*Andromeda polifolia*). To 1 foot. Hardy, deciduous dwarf with creeping root stock. Compact pinkish flowers in nodding terminal umbels in June.

BOX (*Buxus sempervirens*). To 25 feet. Hardy, evergreen; leaves broad below the middle. Often pruned into fantastic shapes.

BOX SAND MYRTLE (*Leiophyllum buxifolium*). To 2 feet. Hardy, evergreen. White, pink flowers in May, June followed by disklike fruit.

BRIDAL WREATH (*Spiraea prunifolia*). To 6 feet. Hardy, deciduous, with white flowers in April, May.

BUCHU (*Diosma ericoides*). To 2 feet. Tender evergreen with a profusion of white flowers May, June. Mild climates only.

BUCKTHORN (*Rhamnus cathartica*). To 12 feet. Hardy, deciduous, with small greenish flowers in June, followed by black fruit.

BUTTERCUP WINTER HAZEL (*Corylopsis pauciflora*). To 6 feet. Semihardy, deciduous, with yellow flowers in April. Winter-protect in North.

BUTTONBUSH (*Cephalanthus occidentalis*). To 20 feet. Hardy, deciduous, with good foliage, attractive creamy flowers July to September. Pretty shrub; moist soil.

CAPE JASMINE (*Gardenia jasminoides*). To 6 feet. Tender evergreen with large, often double, fragrant waxy-white flowers in February. Mild climates only.

CAROLINA CHERRY LAUREL (*Prunus caroliniana*). To 40 feet. Hardy, evergreen. Small, cream-white flowers in April, May. Can be grown in mild climates.

CAROLINA RHODODENDRON (*Rhododendron carolinianum*). To 6 feet. Hardy, evergreen, with large pale rose-purple to white flowers. Good in half shade, moist acid soil.

CARPENTERIA (*Carpenteria californica*). To 10 feet. Tender, evergreen, with stark white fragrant flowers in June, July. Mild climates only.

CHINESE AZALEA (*Rhododendron molle*). To 5 feet. Hardy, deciduous, with golden-yellow flowers in April, May before leaves appear. Grows in half shade, moist acid soil.

CHINESE FRINGE TREE (*Chionanthus retusa*). To 20 feet. Semihardy, deciduous, with showy panicles of white flowers in June, July, followed by dark-blue oval fruit. Protect in North.

CHINESE INDIGO (*Indigofera decora*). To 2 feet. Tender, deciduous. Racemes of pink flowers edged white in July, August. Mild climates only.

CINNAMON CLETHRA (*Clethra acuminata*). To 15 feet. Hardy, deciduous, sweet-scented shrub with white, pinkish flowers in July, September.

CORAL ARDISIA (*Ardisia crispa*). From 2 to 3 feet. Tender, deciduous, with white flower in April, May; coral-red berries that persist for a year or more. Warm climates only.

CORAL COPROSMA (*Coprosma Baueri*). To 25 feet. Tender, evergreen, with small white, greenish flowers in June, followed by yellow fruit. Mild climates only.

CORNELIAN CHERRY (*Cornus mas*). To 20 feet. Hardy, deciduous, with yellow flowers in April, followed by edible scarlet fruit. Tolerates shade.

CRAPE MYRTLE (*Lagerstroemia indica*). To 20 feet. Tender, deciduous, with white, pink, purple flowers in profusion August to October. Beautiful, very popular shrub. Warm climates only.

CROWBERRY (*Empetrum nigrum*). To 10 inches. Hardy, evergreen, with tiny purplish flowers in April, May. Fruit, black, berry-like.

CUTLEAF STEPHANANDRA (*Stephanandra incisa*). To 8 feet. Hardy, deciduous. Grown for its interesting foliage. Flowers white, greenish, in June.

DAHOON (*Ilex Cassine*). To 25 feet. Semihardy, evergreen, with small whitish flowers in May, followed by dull red, sometimes yellow, berries; attractive foliage and showy berries. Protect in North.

DESERT WILLOW (*Chilopsis linearis*). To 20 feet. Tender, deciduous, with lilac yellow-striped flowers, June to September. Blooms when only a few feet high. Dry soil. Warm climates only.

DROOPING ENKIANTHUS (*Enkianthus cernuus var. rubens*). To 15 feet. Hardy, deciduous. Drooping racemes of deep red flowers in May.

DROOPING MELALEUCA (*Melaleuca armillaris*). To 30 feet. Tender, evergreen. Typical "bottle brush" spikes of white flowers on graceful branches. Warm climates only.

DWARF FOTHERGILLA (*Fothergilla Gardeni*). To 3 feet. Hardy, deciduous. Dense beads of white flowers in April before leaves appear, followed by capsular fruit.

EUROPEAN HAZELNUT; FILBERT (*Corylus Avellana*). To 15 feet. Hardy, deciduous, with yellow drooping catkins in March before leaves. Grown for ornament and small edible nuts.

FEBRUARY DAPHNE (*Daphne Mezereum*). To 4 feet. Hardy, deciduous, with lilac-purple flowers appearing in April before leaves. Fruit scarlet.

FIVE-BLADED ARALIA (*Acanthopanax Sieboldianus*). To 10 feet. Hardy, deciduous, with graceful, arching branches; ornamental foliage. Flowers greenish white; fruit a black berry.

FLAME AZALEA (*Rhododendron calendulaceum*). To 10 feet. Deciduous; yellow to scarlet funnellike flowers. Grows in half shade, moist acid soil, in sheltered location. United States.

FLANNEL BUSH (*Fremontia californica*). To 10 feet. Evergreen with yellow flowers in June, July—a favorite California shrub. For warm climates only. Grows in dry soil.

FLOWERING MAPLE (*Abutilon vars.*). From 5 to 10 feet. Nodding Chinese lantern–shaped, orange, red, yellow, white and striped flowers from spring to fall. Not hardy in North.

FLOWERING RASPBERRY (*Rubus odoratus*). To 6 feet. Rose-purple flowers varying to whitish June to September, followed by red fruit (not edible). United States.

FORTUNE FONTANESIA (*Fontanesia Fortunei*). To 15 feet. Hardy, deciduous, with slim panicles of small white flowers in May, June, followed by a flat winged nutlet.

FRANCHET COTONEASTER (*Cotoneaster Franchetii*). To 10 feet. Tender, evergreen, with pinkish flowers in June followed by orange-red fruit. Good for dry soil, sun. Mild climates only.

FRENCH MULBERRY (*Callicarpa americana*). To 6 feet. Tender, deciduous, with bluish flowers, May to July, followed by violet, white fruit. Mild climates only.

FRENCH TAMARIX (*Tamarix gallica*). To 30 feet. Hardy, deciduous, with white or pinkish flowers in July. Excellent for salt air and wind conditions; popular as a windbreak. Seacoast to Midwest.

GARDEN SHADBLOW (*Amelanchier ovalis*). To 8 feet. Hardy, deciduous, with erect racemes of white flowers, followed by small dark-blue or black pome.

GLOSSY ABELIA (*Abelia grandiflora*). To 6 feet. Hardy, semievergreen. Pretty shrub with white, flushed-pink bells June to November.

GOLDEN ST. JOHNS WORT (*Hypericum aureum*). To 4 feet. Hardy, deciduous, with yellow flowers July to August. Popular ornamental for borders, shrubberies, rockeries.

GORSE (*Ulex europaeus*). To 4 feet. Semihardy, deciduous. Looks evergreen because of young green branches. Very spiny. Fragrant yellow flowers in profusion most of the year, followed by dark brown fruit. Good for sandy soils. Protect in North.

GRAY DOGWOOD (*Cornus racemosa*). To 15 feet. Hardy, deciduous, with panicles of white or greenish-white flowers in June, followed by white fruit.

GRECIAN LAUREL (*Laurus nobilis*). To 40 feet. Hardy, evergreen, with yellow flowers in May, followed by black or dark purple fruit.

GROUNDSEL BUSH (*Baccharis halimifolia*). To 12 feet. Hardy, semievergreen. Excellent for coastal regions. Attractive white flowers August, September; fruit, pure white. Particularly good for coast, moist soil.

GUM ROCKROSE (*Cistus ladaniferus*). To 5 feet. Tender, evergreen, with white flowers, petals spotted purple at base in June, July. Mild climates only.

HAIRY PHOTINIA (*Photinia villosa*). To 15 feet. Hardy, deciduous, with white flowers in May followed by red, berrylike fruit.

HAKEA (*Hakea pugioniformis*). To 8 feet. Tender, evergreen, with white flowers in April, May. Mild climates only.

HEATHER (*Calluna vulgaris*). To 3 feet. Hardy, evergreen, with purplish flowers May to July.

HIGHBUSH BLUEBERRY (*Vaccinium corymbosum*). To 15 feet. Hardy, deciduous. Clusters of white or pinkish flowers in May followed by blue-black fruit.

HIMALAYA HONEYSUCKLE (*Leycesteria formosa*). To 6 feet. Semihardy, deciduous. Drooping spikes of purplish flowers in August, September followed by berrylike fruit. Protect in North.

HOLLY MAHONIA (*Mahonia Aquifolium*). To 3 feet. Hardy, evergreen, with yellow flowers in April, followed by navy-blue fruit.

HOLLY OSMANTHUS (*Osmanthus ilicifolius*). To 20 feet. Tender, evergreen. Few large spiny-toothed leaves. Fragrant white flowers in June, July. Warm climates only.

HYDRANGEA, HOUSE (*Hydrangea macrophylla*). To 12 feet. Semihardy, deciduous. Massive flowers blue, pink, white in June, July. Protect in North.

IBOTA PRIVET (*Ligustrum obtusifolium*). To 10 feet. Hardy, deciduous. Nodding panicles of white flowers in June followed by black berrylike fruit.

INDICA AZALEA (*Rhododendron indicum vars., R. Simsii hybrids*). To 6 feet. Hardy, evergreen. Handsome funnel-shaped red, pink-white, lilac, double or single flowers in June, July. Grows in half shade, moist soil.

INKBERRY; WINTERBERRY (*Ilex glabra*). To 8 feet. Semihardy, evergreen. White flowers in June, July, followed by black berries. Protect in North.

JAPANESE AUCUBA (*Aucuba japonica*). To 15 feet. Semihardy, evergreen, with scarlet or sometimes yellow or white fruit in June. Protect in North. Grows in half shade. Dry soil.

JAPANESE BARBERRY (*Berberis Thunbergii*). To 8 feet. Hardy, deciduous, with yellow flowers in April, followed by scarlet fruit. Vigorous, popular.

JAPANESE BEAUTYBERRY (*Callicarpa japonica*). To 5 feet. Hardy, deciduous, with pink, whitish flowers in August, followed by violet, white fruit.

JAPANESE HOLLY (*Ilex crenata*). To 20 feet. Semihardy, evergreen. White flowers in May, June, followed by black berries. Protect in North.

JAPANESE PLUM (*Prunus salicina*). To 25 feet. Hardy, deciduous. White flowers in May, followed by yellow or bright red fruit.

JAPANESE TREE LILAC (*Syringa japonica*). To 30 feet. Hardy, deciduous. Panicles of long yellowish-white flowers in May, June. One of the most popular ornamental shrubs. Moist soil.

JAPANESE WITCH HAZEL (*Hamamelis japonica*). To 30 feet. Hardy, deciduous, with yellow flowers January to March. Moist soil.

JESSAMINE; POET'S JESSAMINE (*Jasminum officinale*). To 30 feet. Tender to semihardy, evergreen. Clusters of fragrant white flowers June to September, followed by black berry fruit. Climbing or with weak stems. For warm climates but withstands climate of near coastal regions of central, eastern states.

JETBEAD (*Rhodotypos tetrapetala*). To 6 feet. Hardy, deciduous, with white flowers in May, June, followed by shining black fruit. Ornamental.

KERRIA (*Kerria japonica*). To 8 feet. Hardy, deciduous, with myriad golden-yellow flowers June to September. Very popular.

KOUSA DOGWOOD (*Cornus Kousa*). To 20 feet. Hardy, deciduous, with white flowers, followed by pinkish fruit.

LABRADOR TEA (*Ledum groenlandicum*). To 3 feet. Hardy, evergreen, with small white flowers in May, June, followed by capsular fruit.

LAMBKILL (*Kalmia angustifolia*). To 3 feet. Hardy, evergreen, with purple or crimson flowers June, July.

LAVENDER COTTON (*Santolina Chamaecyparissus*). To 2 feet. Semihardy, evergreen, with yellow flowers June to August. Low border or edging plant. Protect in North.

LEAD PLANT (*Amorpha canescens*). To 4 feet. Hardy, deciduous, with blue flowers July, August. Ornamental foliage with gray down.

LEATHER LEAF (*Chamaedaphne calyculata*). To 5 feet. Hardy, evergreen, with a profusion of white flowers April to June. Attractive glossy leaves throughout the winter. Moist soil.

LEATHERWOOD (*Cyrilla racemiflora*). To 30 feet. Tender, evergreen, with small white flowers June, July. Mild climates only.

LEATHERWOOD (*Dirca palustris*). To 6 feet. Hardy, deciduous, with yellowish flowers March, April, followed by red or greenish fruit. Shade, moist soil.

LEMON BOTTLEBUSH (*Callistemon lanceolatus*). To 30 feet. Tender, evergreen. Flowers with bright red stamens. Mild climates only.

LEUCOTHOE (*Leucothoe axillaris*). To 6 feet. Semihardy, evergreen. Racemes of white flowers in April, May. Protect in North. Moist soil.

LILAC DAPHNE (*Daphne Genkwa*). To 3 feet. Hardy, deciduous, with clusters of lilac flowers strung along last year's branches in April before leaves appear.

LILY MAGNOLIA (*Magnolia liliflora*). To 10 feet. Hardy, deciduous, flowers purplish outside, white inside, in April, followed by brownish fruit.

MAHALA MAT (*Ceanothus prostratus*). To 1 foot. Tender, evergreen. A west coast favorite with blue flowers in May.

MALEBERRY (*Lyonia ligustrina*). To 12 feet. Hardy, deciduous, with white or pink flowers May to July.

MANCHURIAN LILAC (*Syringa amurensis*). To 12 feet. Hardy, deciduous, with yellowish-white flowers in May, June. Moist soil.

MEXICAN ORANGE (*Choisya ternata*). To 10 feet. Tender, evergreen, with showy, fragrant, white flowers dominating foliage. Mild climates only.

MISTLETOE FAMILY (*Loranthaceae*). Various heights. Hardy, deciduous, with yellowish-green flowers in July, August, followed by clusters of creamy-yellow berries.

MISTLETOE FIG (*Ficus diversifolia*). To 10 feet. Tender, evergreen. Pretty, often grown as pot plant. Yellow fruit. Mild climates only.

MONGOLIAN DEUTZIA (*Deutzia parviflora*). To 6 feet. Hardy, deciduous, with white flowers in May.

MONTEVIDEO ESCALLONIA (*Escallonia montevidensis*). To 9 feet. Tender, evergreen, with white flowers in May, June. Robust rapid grower. Mild climates only.

MOTHER OF THYME; CREEPING THYME (*Thymus Serpyllum*). To 6 inches. Hardy, evergreen. Prostrate subshrub. Purplish flowers June to September. Many varieties in many colors—white, yellow, red, rose.

MOUNTAIN ANDROMEDA (*Pieris floribunda*). To 6 feet. Hardy, evergreen, with white flowers in April, May, followed by capsulelike fruit.

MOUNTAIN HOLLY (*Nemopanthus mucronata*). To 10 feet. Hardy, deciduous, with whitish flowers in May followed by red fruit. Beautiful autumn foliage. Moist soil.

MOUNTAIN LAUREL (*Kalmia latifolia*). To 10 feet. Hardy, evergreen, with rose flowers, purple to white inside, in May, June.

MOUNTAIN ROSE BAY (*Rhododendron catawbiense*). To 20 feet. Hardy, evergreen, with broad bell-shaped, lilac-purple flowers in May, June. Grows in half shade, moist soil.

MOUNTAIN SNOWBERRY (*Symphoricarpos oreophilus*). To 5 feet. Hardy, deciduous, with pinkish flowers in June, July, followed by white or pinkish fruit.

NANDINA (*Nandina domestica*). To 8 feet. Semihardy evergreen with white flowers in June, July, followed by small bright red berries; leaves turn red in fall. Protect in North.

NEW JERSEY TEA (*Ceanothus americanus*). To 3 feet. Hardy, deciduous, with white flowers July to September.

NINEBARK (*Physocarpus vars.*). From 3 to 20 feet. Hardy, deciduous, with white or pinkish flowers in May, June.

OLEASTER (*Elaeagnus angustifolia*). To 20 feet. Hardy, deciduous, with inconspicuous fragrant flowers in June, followed by yellow, silvery fruit. United States.

OTAKSA HYDRANGEA (*Hydrangea macrophylla var. otaksa*). To 10 feet. Semihardy, deciduous. Dwarf blue, pink, white flowers in June, July. Protect in North.

PAGODA DOGWOOD (*Cornus alternifolia*). To 25 feet. Hardy, deciduous, with white or greenish flowers in July followed by dark-blue, sometimes yellow, fruit.

PALE BROOM (*Cytisus albus*). To 1 foot. Hardy, deciduous, with yellow flowers June to August.

PAPAW (*Asimina triloba*). To 30 feet. Hardy, deciduous, with purple flowers in March, April, followed by brown fruit in October.

PERSIAN PARROTIA (*Parrotia persica*). To 15 feet. Hardy, deciduous, with purplish flowers in March, April, before leaves appear.

PURPLE CHOKEBERRY (*Aronia atropurpurea*). To 12 feet. Hardy, deciduous, with white, pinkish flowers in May, followed by purple-black fruit.

REDBUD PEARL BUSH (*Exochorda Giraldii*). To 15 feet. Hardy, deciduous, highly ornamental with white flowers in April, May.

REDVEIN ENKIANTHUS (*Enkianthus campanulatus*). From 8 to 20 feet. Hardy, deciduous. A handsome, erect shrub with drooping pale yellow or pale orange flowers marked red in May, June. Likes sheltered location, peaty soil.

RHODORA (*Rhododendron canadense*). To 3 feet. Hardy, deciduous, with clusters of rose-purple flowers (sometimes white) in April, May. Grows in half shade, moist to wet acid soil.

ROCK COTONEASTER (*Cotoneaster horizontalis*). To 3 feet. Hardy, semievergreen, with pinkish flowers in June, followed by red fruit. Good as background for rocky spots. Well-drained, dry soil; sun.

ROCK SPIREA (*Holodiscus discolor*). To 20 feet. Hardy, deciduous, with creamy-white flowers in July.

ROSE ACACIA (*Robinia hispida*). To 9 feet. Hardy, deciduous, with bristly, hairy leaflets. Flowers rose or pale purple in May, June.

ROSE BAY RHODODENDRON (*Rhododendron maximum*). To 35 feet. Hardy, evergreen, with rose-spotted green, bell-shaped flowers in June, July. Half shade, moist soil.

ROSE DAPHNE (*Daphne Cneorum*). To 1 foot. Hardy, trailing, evergreen, with pink, fragrant flowers April to September.

ROUNDLEAF COTONEASTER (*Cotoneaster rotundifolia*). To 8 feet. Hardy, deciduous, with white flowers in May, June, followed by red fruit. Good for dry soil, sun.

SALMON BARBERRY (*Berberis aggregata*). To 10 feet. Hardy, deciduous, with pale yellow flowers in April, followed by red fruit.

SALT TREE (*Halimodendron halodendron*). To 6 feet. Hardy, deciduous, with pale purple flowers in May. Very ornamental.

SAND CHERRY (*Prunus Besseyi*). To 3 feet. Hardy, deciduous, with white flowers in May, followed by black, edible fruit.

SARGENT BARBERRY (*Berberis Sargentiana*). To 6 feet. Tender, evergreen, with clusters of yellow flowers in April, followed by bluish-black fruit. Mild climates only.

SCARLET FIRETHORN (*Pyracantha coccinea*). To 20 feet. Semihardy, evergreen, with white flowers in May, June, followed by red or orange fruit. For South and central states.

SCORPION SENNA (*Coronilla Emerus*). To 9 feet. Hardy, deciduous, with yellow flowers in May, June.

SCOTCH BROOM (*Cytisus scorparius*). To 10 feet. Hardy, deciduous, with yellow flowers in May, June.

SEA BUCKTHORN (*Hippophae rhamnoides*). To 30 feet. Hardy, deciduous, with inconspicuous yellow flowers in April, followed by orange-yellow fruit persisting through winter.

SHRUB ALTHEA (*Hibiscus syriacus*). To 12 feet. Hardy, deciduous shrub good for city conditions. Can be trained to a tree. Flowers: rose, purple to white, bluish, in August.

SIBERIAN PEA TREE (*Caragana arborescens*). To 20 feet. Hardy, deciduous, with yellow flowers in May, June. Makes good tall hedge, too.

SLENDER DEUTZIA (*Deutzia gracilis*). To 6 feet. Hardy, deciduous, with graceful white flowers in May.

SMOOTH HYDRANGEA (*Hydrangea arborescens*). To 10 feet. Fairly hardy, deciduous, popular, with white flowers in June, July. Best to protect in North.

SMOOTH SWEETSHRUB (*Calycanthus fertilis*). To 10 feet. Hardy, deciduous, with reddish-brown flowers in June, July.

SNOWBERRY (*Symphoricarpos albus*). To 3 feet. Hardy, deciduous, with bell-shaped pinkish flowers June to September, followed by snow-white fruit.

SOUTHERN BUSH HONEYSUCKLE (*Diervilla sessilifolia*). To 5 feet. Hardy, deciduous, with yellow flowers, sometimes shaded reddish or brownish in June, July.

SPICE BUSH (*Benzoin aestivalis*). To 15 feet. Hardy, deciduous, with greenish-yellow flowers in March before leaves, followed by scarlet fruit. Leaves turn colorful yellow in autumn. Moist soil.

SPIKE BROOM (*Cytisus nigricans*). To 4 feet. Hardy, deciduous, with yellow flowers in July, August. Ideal for edging other shrubs.

SPIREA (*Spiraea vars.*). From 1 to 12 feet. Hardy, deciduous. A wide variety of vigorous ornamental shrubs with white or pink flowers April to September. United States.

SPREADING COTONEASTER (*Cotoneaster divaricata*). To 6 feet. Hardy, deciduous, with pinkish flowers followed by bright red fruit. Good for dry soil. Sun.

SPRING HEATH (*Erica carnea*). To 1 foot. Hardy, evergreen, with red flowers March to May.

STAGGER BUSH (*Lyonia mariana*). To 6 feet. Hardy, deciduous, with white or pinkish flowers in May, June.

SUMMER LILAC (*Buddleia Davidii*). To 15 feet. Hardy, deciduous, with lilac, orange-eyed flowers in profusion July to September.

SWEET AZALEA (*Rhododendron arborescens*). To 10 feet. Hardy, deciduous, with white or pinkish flowers in June, July. Leaves turn red; protect against wind. Half shade, moist soil.

SWEET BROOM (*Cytisus fragrans*). From 3 to 4 feet. Hardy, deciduous, with white, fragrant flowers June to August. A very showy plant. Sun.

SWEET FERN (*Comptonia asplenifolia*). To 5 feet. Hardy, deciduous, with inconspicuous flowers in June, fernlike leaves.

SWEET PEPPERBUSH (*Clethra alnifolia*). To 10 feet. Hardy, deciduous, with pink-tinged white flowers July to September.

SWEET SPIRE (*Itea virginica*). To 10 feet. Hardy, deciduous, with white, fragrant flowers in July, foliage turning red in late summer.

TAPER-POINTED COTONEASTER (*Cotoneaster acuminata*). To 12 feet. Hardy, deciduous, with pinkish flowers in June, followed by bright red fruit. Good for dry soil, sun.

TATARIAN DOGWOOD (*Cornus alba*). To 10 feet. Hardy, deciduous, with white or greenish-white flowers in May, June. Fruit whitish, bluish; bright red branches.

TRIFOLIATE ORANGE (*Poncirus trifoliata*). To 6 feet. Tender to semihardy, deciduous, with white flowers in April, followed by small aromatic orange-like fruit. Hardy to Philadelphia if protected. Best in mild climates.

TRUE DWARF BOX (*Buxus sempervirens var. suffruticosa*). From 2 to 8 feet. Hardy, evergreen, dwarf with small leaves.

WASHINGTON THORN (*Crataegus Phaenopyrum*). To 30 feet. Hardy, deciduous, highly ornamental with white flowers in May, followed by red fruit.

WINGED EUONYMUS (*Euonymus alatus*). To 8 feet. Hardy, deciduous, with greenish flowers in May, purplish fruit, crimson foliage in autumn.

WITCH HAZEL (*Hamamelis virginiana*). To 15 feet. Hardy, deciduous. Yellow flowers in September. Handsome shrub for late summer bloom.

YEDDO HAWTHORN (*Raphiolepis umbellata*). To 12 feet. Tender, evergreen. Dense panicles of fragrant white flowers in April, May. Mild climates only.

YELLOWEDGE CALIFORNIA PRIVET (*Ligustrum ovalifolium var. aureo-marginatum*). To 15 feet. Hardy, half-evergreen, with white flowers edged with yellow. Commonly used for hedges.

More Trees

AMERICAN BEECH (*Fagus grandifolia*). To 100 feet. Hardy, deciduous, with bright yellow leaves in autumn.

AMERICAN ELM (*Ulmus americana*). To 120 feet. Hardy, deciduous, with inconspicuous flowers turning into flat nutlets. A favorite shade tree.

AMERICAN HOP HORNBEAM (*Ostrya virginiana*). To 60 feet. Hardy, deciduous, with hoplike fruit somewhat like that of the elm.

AMERICAN HORNBEAM (*Carpinus caroliniana*). To 40 feet. Hardy, deciduous, with green fruit. Often planted for use as tall hedge.

AMERICAN LINDEN (*Tilia americana*). To 120 feet. Hardy, deciduous, with creamy flowers, nutlike greenish fruit.

AMERICAN REDBUD (*Cercis canadensis*). To 40 feet. Hardy, deciduous. Rapid grower; bright-rose flowers in May, later turning brown.

AMUR CORK TREE (*Phellodendron amurense*). To 50 feet. Hardy, deciduous, with green-white flowers in June, conspicuous black berries in autumn.

AVOCADO (*Persea americana*). To 60 feet. Tender, evergreen; grown for its delicious, green, fleshy fruit—the avocado pear. Mild climates only.

BALD CYPRESS (*Taxodium distichum*). To 150 feet. Hardy, deciduous, with light green leaves that turn a terra-cotta orange in fall.

BUTTERNUT (*Juglans cinerea*). To 100 feet. Hardy, deciduous, ornamental, often grown for its edible nuts.

BUTTONWOOD (*Platanus occidentalis*). To 150 feet. Hardy, deciduous. Stands shearing well; good for restricted areas. Likes moist soil.

CAJEPUT TREE (*Melaleuca Leucadendra*). To 20 feet. Tender, evergreen, with conspicuous handsome white flowers. Mild climates only.

CALIFORNIA INCENSE CEDAR (*Libocedrus decurrens*). To 100 feet. Semihardy, evergreen, with bright green foliage.

Looks much like arbor vitae. Protect in North.

CAMPHOR TREE (*Cinnamomum Camphora*). To 40 feet. Tender evergreen, unusual and interesting. Buds of yellow flowers enclosed by large, overlapping scales. Likes dry soil. For South only.

CAROLINA HEMLOCK (*Tsuga caroliniana*). To 75 feet. Semihardy, evergreen, graceful, lacy. Flat leaves banded white underneath. A valuable ornamental tree. Protect in North.

CHINESE ELM (*Ulmus parvifolia*). To 45 feet. Hardy; deciduous in cold climates, evergreen in mild climates. Inconspicuous clusters of flowers turning to flat nutlet. A very useful elm.

CHINESE JUNIPER (*Juniperus chinensis*). To 60 feet. Hardy, evergreen, a favorite tree.

CLAMMY LOCUST (*Robinia viscosa*). To 40 feet. Hardy, deciduous, with sticky twigs. Pink flowers in May, June, turning to pea-shaped pods.

CUCUMBER TREE (*Magnolia acuminata*). To 100 feet. Hardy, deciduous, with white flowers in May. Fruit brownish, cucumber-shaped.

FALSE ACACIA (*Robinia Pseudo-Acacia*). To 80 feet. Hardy, deciduous, with delicate, lacy foliage, white, fragrant flowers turning to reddish brown pods.

FALSE CYPRESS (*Chamaecyparis vars.*). To 100 feet. Hardy, evergreen, with highly scented yellow or red flowers.

FLOWERING ASH (*Fraxinus Ornus*). To 60 feet. Hardy, deciduous, with fragrant white flowers. Favorite avenue or ornamental tree. Transplants easily.

FRAGRANT EPAULETTE TREE (*Pterostyrax hispida Pyrus*). To 50 feet. Hardy, deciduous, with interesting clusters of white flowers.

FRASER MAGNOLIA (*Magnolia Fraseri*). To 50 feet. Hardy, deciduous, with white flowers, rosy fruit.

GOAT WILLOW (*Salix Caprea*). To 25 feet. Hardy, deciduous, excellent shade, screen, ornamental tree. Flowers appear before leaves.

GOLDEN CHAIN (*Laburnum anagyroides*). To 30 feet. Hardy, deciduous, outstanding tree with yellow flowers.

GOLDENRAIN TREE (*Koelreuteria paniculata*). To 30 feet. Hardy, deciduous. Superb small tree with yellow flowers, followed by bronze pods.

GUAYMOCHIL (*Pithecellobium dulce*). To 50 feet. Tender, evergreen; with white flowers. Mild climates only.

HACKBERRY (*Celtis occidentalis*). To 120 feet. Hardy, deciduous. Excellent ornamental and shade tree.

HAWTHORN (*Crataegus vars.*). From 15 to 30 feet. Hardy, deciduous. Highly ornamental; white blooms, red fruit.

HERCULES'-CLUB (*Aralia spinosa*). To 30 feet. Hardy, deciduous; fruit attractive to birds.

HONEY LOCUST (*Gleditsia triacanthos*). To 140 feet. Tender, deciduous. Excellent specimen and shade tree.

HORSE CHESTNUT (*Aesculus Hippocastanum*). To 100 feet. Hardy, deciduous. Notable, persistent, cream flower clusters in spring.

JACARANDA (*Jacaranda*). To 50 feet. Superb tropical tree with long panicles of blue flowers. Mild climates only.

JAPANESE PAGODA TREE (*Sophora japonica*). To 80 feet. Hardy, deciduous, well-known avenue tree, with light yellow flowers followed by pealike fruit.

JAPANESE SNOWBELL (*Styrax japonica*). To 30 feet. Hardy, deciduous, small, compact, beautiful, with fragrant white flowers.

JAPANESE STEWARTIA (*Stewartia Pseudo-Camellia*). To 50 feet. Hardy, deciduous, with superb white flowers with orange anthers in July.

JERUSALEM THORN (*Parkinsonia aculeata*). To 30 feet. Tender, deciduous, with yellow flowers. Also makes good hedge. For South only.

KATSURA TREE (*Cercidiphyllum japonicum*). From 20 to 100 feet. Hardy, deciduous, with inconspicuous flowers; flamboyant yellow or scarlet leaves in fall. Likes moist soil.

KENTUCKY COFFEE TREE (*Gymnocladus dioica*). To 100 feet. Semihardy (to Massachusetts), deciduous. An excellent specimen tree.

LARGE-LEAVED CUCUMBER TREE (*Magnolia macrophylla*). To 50 feet. Hardy, deciduous, with highly ornamental fragrant white flowers.

LINDEN (*Tilia vulgaris*). To 120 feet. Hardy, deciduous, with pendant clusters of white, yellowish flowers. Fruit nutlike. Favorite avenue tree.

LOBLOLLY BAY (*Gordonia Lasianthus*). To 60 feet. Tender, evergreen, with white flowers. For South only.

LOFTY FIG (*Ficus altissima*). To 50 feet. Tender, evergreen, wide-spreading. For mild climates only.

LOQUAT (*Eriobotrya japonica*). To 20 feet. Tender, evergreen, with white flowers, followed by yellow pear-shaped fruit. Tolerates shade. For mild climates only.

MANGO (*Mangifera indica*). To 90 feet. Tender, evergreen, with pinkish-white flowers in April. Tasty, yellow-reddish fruit. For mild climates only.

MASSANGE DRACAENA (*Dracaena fragrans vars. Massangeana*). To 20 feet. Tender, evergreen, grown for its decorative foliage. Leaves have broad yellow stripes down center. Unimportant, yellowish flowers.

MOUNTAIN EBONY (*Bauhinia variegata var. candida*). To 20 feet. Tender, evergreen, with white flowers. For mild climates only.

NAIBEL (*Hesperethusa crenulata*). To 25 feet. Tender, evergreen. A large tree with unusual conical habit. For mild climates only.

NORFOLK ISLAND PINE (*Araucaria excelsa*). From 160 to 200 feet. Tender, evergreen. A large tree with unusual conical habit. For mild climates only.

OAK (*Quercus vars.*). Various heights. Deciduous species hardy in North. Evergreen species for South only.

ORANGE, LEMON, LIME, CITRON (*Citrus*). Various heights. Tender, evergreen, with white or pink flowers, usually exceedingly fragrant, followed by their respective fruits. For mild climates only.

ORIENTAL PLANE TREE (*Platanus orientalis*). To 100 feet. Hardy, deciduous, likes moist soil. Transplants easily, takes pruning. A useful lawn tree, not often seen in the United States.

PEPPERIDGE (*Nyssa sylvatica*). To 100 feet. Hardy, deciduous, ornamental tree. Likes moist soil.

POPLAR (*Populus vars.*). To 100 feet. Hardy, deciduous trees and shrubs. Highly ornamental; excellent for windbreaks.

PURPLE BAUHINIA (*Bauhinia purpurea*). To 6 feet. Tender, evergreen. Excellent ornamental for warm climates, with red or white flowers.

PUSSY WILLOW (*Salix discolor*). To 20 feet. Hardy, deciduous, with familiar flowers in dense silvery, downy catkins.

RED CEDAR (*Juniperus virginiana*). To 100 feet. Hardy, evergreen. Rich dark foliage, bluish fruit.

ROSE APPLE (*Eugenia Jambos*). To 30 feet. Tender, evergreen, with greenish-white flowers, greenish-yellow fruit. Very showy stamens. Mild climates only.

ROYAL PAULOWNIA (*Paulownia tomentosa*). To 40 feet. Semihardy, deciduous, with pale violet flowers. Best protect in North.

RUBBER PLANT (*Ficus elastica*). To 20 feet. Tender, evergreen, with thick glossy leaves; also a favorite pot and tub plant. For mild climates only.

SCARLET DOMBEYA (*Dombeya Wallichii*). To 30 feet. Tender, evergreen. Large, pendulous, dense heads of scarlet or pink flowers. For mild climates only.

SILK OAK (*Grevillea robusta*). To 150 feet. Tender, deciduous, with orange flowers. A rapid grower. For mild climates only.

SOURWOOD (*Oxydendrum arboreum*). To 60 feet. Hardy, deciduous, very ornamental, with white flowers.

SWEET BAY (*Magnolia virginiana*). To 60 feet. Tender, half-evergreen, with white flowers, followed by red fruit. For mild climates only.

SWEET GUM (*Liquidambar Styraciflua*). To 140 feet. Tender, deciduous, with leaves turning red in fall. For mild climates only.

TAMARIND (*Tamarindus indica*). To 80 feet. Tender, evergreen; massive, highly ornamental. Bears light yellow flowers, followed by rust-brown fruit. Likes moist soil. For mild climates.

TREE-OF-HEAVEN (*Ailanthus altissima*). To 60 feet. Hardy, deciduous, resistant to smoke and dry air of cities. A rapid grower.

TULIP TREE (*Liriodendron Tulipifera*). To 200 feet. Hardy, deciduous, one of the most handsome native trees. Chartreuse flowers tinged orange at base, followed by brown fruit. Likes moist soil.

UMBRELLA PINE (*Sciadopitys verticillata*). To 120 feet. Hardy, evergreen, with dark green leaves in umbrellalike whorls, highly ornamental.

UMBRELLA TREE (*Magnolia tripetala*). To 40 feet. Hardy, deciduous, with white flowers, followed by rose fruit.

WEEPING BEECH (*Fagus sylvatica var. pendula*). To 40 feet. Hardy, deciduous, with attractive characteristically irregular growth, gracefully drooping branches. Bears brown edible nuts. Excellent for large areas.

WEEPING MULBERRY (*Morus alba pendula*). To 50 feet. Hardy, deciduous, with typically weeping branches.

WESTERN CATALPA (*Catalpa speciosa*). To 100 feet. Hardy, deciduous. Favorite lawn and avenue tree. White flowers, spotted brown.

WHITE FRINGE TREE (*Chionanthus virginica*). To 30 feet. Hardy, deciduous. Useful low tree or shrub with white flowers followed by navy-blue fruit.

WHITE LINDEN (*Tilia tomentosa*). To 100 feet. Hardy, deciduous. Excellent ornamental tree with fragrant pale yellow flowers.

YELLOW WOOD (*Cladrastis lutea*). To 50 feet. Hardy, deciduous, with fragrant white flowers, followed by pealike fruit in June.

YEW (*Taxus vars.*). Various heights. Hardy, evergreen, of various habits useful for many diverse purposes. Flowers and seeds in berrylike red cups.

YULAN (*Magnolia denudata*). To 50 feet. Hardy, with white flowers, brownish fruit.

More Hedges
(To 2 FEET)

ALPINE CURRANT (*Ribes alpinum*). Excellent hedge for shade; hardy to extreme North. Deciduous, but leaves appear very early in spring.

ALPINE FLOWERING QUINCE (*Chaenomeles japonica alpina*). Obliging low hedge that bears orange-scarlet flowers even when clipped. Hardy in North, deciduous.

BARBERRY VERRUCULOSA (*Berberis verruculosa compacta*). Low, spiny, glossy-leaved evergreen, with golden yellow flowers, black fruit. Does not require shearing. Eventually will grow to 3 feet.

BIGLEAF WINTERCREEPER (*Euonymus Fortunei vegetus*). Hardy, evergreen with large handsome leaves, very good for shade.

BOX BARBERRY (*Berberis Thunbergii minor*). An excellent slow growing form of *B. Thunbergii* which can be maintained as low as 6 inches high by shearing. Hardy to extreme North, deciduous.

BOXLEAF BURNINGBRUSH (*Euonymus japonicus microphyllus*). Evergreen with glossy, good-textured leaves; of handsome, compact growth. Good for South and California.

BREATH OF HEAVEN (*Diosma ericoides*). Tender evergreen, favorite for South and California. Very bushy fine-textured foliage; perfumed white flowers in profusion.

BROADLEAF PERNETTYA; CHILEON PERNETTYA (*Pernettya mucronata*). Evergreen with noticeable, persistent, bright red fruit if not clipped (other colors also available). For the South and California.

CUSHION JAPANESE YEW (*Taxus cuspidata densa*). The most compact, dense, low-growing yew. Hardy, evergreen.

DWARF ALBERTA SPRUCE (*Picea glauca conica*). Good evergreen of narrow conical habit but foliage apt to winter-burn. Hardy to extreme North.

DWARF BORDER FORSYTHIA (*Forsythia intermedia nana*). Hardy, deciduous, good where thick dense hedge desired.

DWARF CRANBERRYBUSH (*Viburnum Opulus nanum*). Hardy, deciduous, of nicely mounded habit.

DWARF ENGLISH YEW (*Taxus baccata repandens*). Nearly prostrate with bluish-green leaves. Hardiest of English yews. Evergreen favorite for the South and California, too. Prefers shade.

DWARF HEDGE YEW; GROUND HEMLOCK (*Taxus canadensis stricta*). Excellent evergreen for shady locations. A favorite in the North and Northwest.

DWARF MYRTLE (*Myrtus communis minima*). Good compact evergreen with substantial foliage. For the South and California.

DWARF NINEBARK (*Physocarpus opulifolius nanus*). Deciduous, thick, twiggy, dense; hardy to extreme North.

DWARF POMEGRANATE (*Punica granatum nana*). Handsome evergreen with pretty leaves, scarlet fruit. For the South and California.

DWARF PURPLE OSIER WILLOW (*Salix purpurea nana*). Deciduous, ideally suited to north and northwest climates, although sometimes injured by snow.

FLOWERING QUINCE (*Chaenomeles lagenaria, Cydonia japonica*). An unusual attractive hedge that can be kept compact, with scarlet flowers in spring before leaves. Hardy, deciduous.

GERMANDER (*Teucrium Chamaedrys*). Semihardy, deciduous, with attractive grayish foliage.

GLOSSY WINTERCREEPER (*Euonymus Fortunei Carrierei*). Hardy evergreen of upright habit; excellent for shade.

GREEN GLOBE ARBOR VITAE (*Thuja occidentalis pumila*). Dwarf dense evergreen, favorite of North and Northwest, although often winter-burned in exposed places.

HINOKI CYPRESS (*Chamaecyparis obtusa gracilis*). Hardy evergreen of compact pyramidal form with rich dark green foliage. Will take light shearing.

JAPANESE BARBERRY (*Berberis Thunbergii*). Very hardy. Deciduous, with bright red fruit. Thrives in almost any soil, stands part shade, even city conditions. Compact, generally needs no shearing.

JAPANESE YEW (*Taxus cuspidata nana*). Hardy evergreen, forms low broad shrubby hedge. One of the best adapted to city conditions.

KINGSVILLE DWARF BOXWOOD (*Buxus microphylla compacta*). The most compact dwarf boxwood. Hardy, evergreen, good for North and Northwest.

KOREAN LITTLELEAF BOXWOOD (*Buxus microphylla koreana*). One of the best boxwoods for North and Northwest although foliage subject to winter-burn. Evergreen.

LODENSE PRIVET (*Ligustrum vulgare lodense*). Excellent. Most dwarf of the dwarf privets. Hardy, deciduous.

MENTOR BARBERRY (*Berberis mentorensis*). An excellent compact semievergreen hybrid, with thick leathery dark-green leaves. Formidable thorns and dull wine-red fruit. Fairly hardy in North, stands heat and drought of South and Southwest.

MUGHO PINE (*Pinus Mugo Mughus*). Evergreen of neat habit, hardy in extreme North. Requires little or no clipping.

OVALLEAF JAPANESE SPIRAEA (*Spiraea japonica ovalifolia*). Hardy, deciduous, with fine-textured foliage, typical white flowers.

PYGMY PEASHRUB (*Caragana pygmaea*). Deciduous, hardy to extreme North but subject to breakage by heavy snows.

SHINYLEAF HONEYSUCKLE (*Lonicera nitida*). Evergreen of fine-textured foliage, dense, thick. Good for South and California.

SLENDER DEUTZIA (*Deutzia gracilis*). Deciduous, hardy, one of the prettiest and most graceful Deutzias. Makes a compact low shrub of arching branches covered with delicate snow-white flowers in May.

SPIRAEA ANTHONY WATERER (*Spiraea Bumalda Anthony Waterer*). Attractive low-growing hybrid with heads of crimson flowers in summer. Deciduous, hardy.

SPREADING ENGLISH YEW (*Taxus baccata repandens*). A favorite evergreen for the South and California. Prefers shade.

TRUE DWARF BOX; EDGINGBOX (*Buxus sempervirens suffruticosa*). Slow-growing hardy dwarf evergreen widely used for low hedges in United States.

TRUE HEDGE COLUMBERRY (*Berberis Thunbergii erecta*). Excellent slim, dense, erect hedge for North and Northwest. Deciduous.

WINTERCREEPER (*Euonymus Fortunei radicans*). Hardy evergreen, excellent for shady locations.

More Hedges
(2 TO 5 FEET)

AMERICAN ARBOR VITAE (*Thuja occidentalis*). One of the best evergreen hedges, hardy to extreme North although foliage subject to winter-burn. Stands shearing well. In the south *Thuja orientalis* does better.

AMERICAN HOLLY (*Ilex opaca*). Hardy evergreen, popular throughout most of the country. Also suitable for tall hedge; attractive foliage, bright-red fruit.

AMUR PRIVET (*Ligustrum amurense*). Sturdy, quick-growing, stands sun or shade. Hardy to extreme North. Not as thick or leafy as **California Privet** (*L. ovalifolium*), but much hardier. Deciduous to semievergreen.

BOXWOOD (*Buxus sempervirens*). Famous evergreen hedging box, a favorite of the South and California. Thrives in partial shade. Semihardy, should be winter protected in New York and central New England.

BUCKTHORN (*Rhamnus cathartica*). Stand-by for middle to tall hedges in cold climates for semishade location. Makes dense hedge of dull-green leaves. Deciduous, hardy to extreme North.

CALIFORNIA PRIVET (*Ligustrum ovalifolium*). Deciduous to half evergreen, the most vigorous common privet with glossy leaves that take well to constant shearing. Not reliable in northernmost states.

CHINESE LILAC (*Syringa chinensis*). Excellent middle to tall hedge plant with fine textured foliage. Deciduous, hardy to extreme North.

CUTLEAF STEPHANANDRA (*Stephanandra incisa*). Deciduous hardy, makes graceful informal hedge. Arching branches with dense, bright-green deeply-lobed leaves.

DEUTZIA LEMOINEI (*Deutzia Lemoinei*). Hardy vigorous hybrid with large leaves, pure white flowers. Nicely shaped. Deciduous.

DWARF JAPANESE YEW (*Taxus cuspidata nana*). Hardy evergreen with dense dark-green wide-spreading foliage. Does well in North. Prefers shade.

DWARF WINGED EUONYMUS (*Euonymus alatus compactus*). Low, compact with foliage turning red in fall. Deciduous, good for North and Northwest.

ENGLISH CHERRY LAUREL (*Prunus Laurocerasus*). Excellent evergreen for warm climates. Stands pruning well.

ENGLISH HOLLY (*Ilex Aquifolium*). Spiny impenetrable evergreen for warm climates, with dense lustrous foliage, scarlet berries.

GLOSSY ABELIA (*Abelia grandiflora*). Evergreen in the South and California; semievergreen in North. Shiny fine-textured foliage with shell-pink flowers.

GLOSSY BUCKTHORN (*Rhamnus Frangula*). Deciduous, hardy, with attractive glossy foliage. Also good for tall hedges. Does well in North.

GLOSSY PRIVET (*Ligustrum lucidum*). A favorite evergreen privet for warm climates. Has long shiny leaves 4 to 6 inches long.

HARDY ORANGE (*Poncirus trifoliata, Citrus trifoliata*). Deciduous. Semihardy (to Philadelphia with winter protection). Bears bright orange fruit on typically spiny branches.

HEDGE COTONEASTER (*Cotoneaster lucida*). A favorite deciduous hedge in the North. Good rich green foliage. Stands shearing well.

HEDGE PRINSEPIA (*Prinsepia uniflora*). Thorny, deciduous, hardy. Dark-green foliage of good substance, white flowers.

HICK'S YEW (*Taxus media Hicksii*). An upright-growing yew with erect, hardy, dark green branches. Evergreen.

JAPANESE BARBERRY (*Berberis Thunbergii*). Most popular hedge next to privet because of its ability to grow in poor soil, partial shade, even in city conditions. Naturally compact, foliage turns red in fall. Deciduous, hardy to extreme North.

JAPANESE QUINCE (*Chaenomeles lagenaria*). An attractive unusual hedge with excellent foliage, scarlet flowers in spring before leaves appear. Hardy to Massachusetts. Deciduous; good for North and Northwest.

JAPANESE YEW (*Taxus cuspidata*). An excellent evergreen hedge for shade with dense dark-green foliage. One of the best evergreens for city conditions. Hardy to extreme North. Likes shade.

KOREAN BARBERRY (*Berberis koreana*). Hardy, deciduous, with red leaves in fall, bright red fruit.

LANTANA (*Lantana Camara*). Colorful tender evergreen for South and California.

Red, orange, pink, lavender flowers; blooms even when clipped. Very tolerant, easy to grow.

LAURESTINUS (*Viburnum Tinus*). A very luxuriant evergreen for the South and California. Of dense habit; stands shade.

LITTLE LEAF JAPANESE HOLLY (*Ilex crenata microphylla*). A smaller variety of **Japanese Holly** with glossy, evergreen, fine-textured foliage. More hardy, more compact, singularly pest-free. For South and California.

MENTOR BARBERRY (*Berberis mentorensis*). Hardy, deciduous, with persistent foliage, attractive dull red fruit. Makes good even growth, needs little clipping.

MOUNTAIN NINEBARK (*Physocarpus monogynus*). Deciduous, hardy to extreme North. Dense spiraealike with white or pinkish flowers when unpruned.

NATAL PLUM (*Carissa grandiflora*). Dense, spiny, tropical evergreen for warm climates. Fragrant white flowers, edible red fruit if not sheared. Takes to shearing well.

PEKING COTONEASTER (*Cotoneaster acutifolia*). Deciduous, hardy to extreme North. Of good, substantial foliage.

PRIVET; PRIM (*Ligustrum vulgare*). Many varieties of deciduous hardy shrubs, some variegated, white, or yellow. Usually flower June, July, if not pruned, followed by black fruit in fall. Grows to about 15 feet.

REGEL'S PRIVET (*Ligustrum obtusifolium Regelianum*). Hardy to extreme North. Deciduous. Makes handsome impenetrable hedge with graceful, horizontally spreading branches.

SAWARA CYPRESS (*Chamaecyparis pisifera filifera*). Hardy evergreen of dense compact habit. Shears well but slender pendulous branches liable to damage in exposed places in North.

SWISS MOUNTAIN PINE (*Pinus Mugo*). Hardy, evergreen, of unpredictable habit. Be sure to match plants carefully upon purchasing.

TOBIRA; JAPANESE PITHOS (*Pittosporum Tobira*). Evergreen for warm climates. Excellent dense hedge with thick leathery leaves, some variegated white.

TRUE MYRTLE; CLASSIC MYRTLE (*Myrtus communis*). Makes beautiful dense hedge. Shiny, evergreen, strongly scented foliage. For warm regions only.

WAYFARING TREE (*Viburnum lantana*). Hardy to extreme North. Deciduous. Prunes well, makes good dense hedge to the ground.

WINGED EUONYMUS (*Euonymus alatus*). A twiggy euonymus, very handsome in fall when leaves turn rose-scarlet. Deciduous, good for North and Northwest.

WINTERGREEN (*Berberis Julianae*). Spiny evergreen shrub with clusters of yellow flowers followed by black purplish fruit. Does not like too heavy pruning. Fairly hardy to New York.

More Hedges
(OVER 5 FEET)

AMERICAN BEECH (*Fagus grandifolia*). Deciduous, hardy to extreme North. Excellent ornamental tree with smooth light bark, blue-green leaves that turn yellow in autumn.

AMUR CHOKEBERRY; RACEMOSE CHERRY (*Prunus Maackii*). Deciduous, hardy to extreme North. Good dense hedge, one of the earliest to leaf.

AMUR MAPLE (*Acer Ginnala*). Graceful shrub or tree to 20 feet. Deciduous, hardy to extreme North. Makes tall dense hedge. Foliage colors brightly in fall. Panicles of fragrant flowers.

AMUR PRIVET (*Ligustrum amurense*). **Glossy Privet** (*L. lucidum*). **California Privet** (*L. ovalifolium*). **Privet** (*L. vulgare*). See under hedges 2 to 5 feet.

ARALIA PENTAPHYLLUS (*Acanthopanax Sieboldianus*). Hardy to Massachusetts. Deciduous shrub with graceful arching branches, greenish-white flowers. Tolerant of poor soil and shade, city conditions, but prune lightly.

AUSTRALIAN BRUSHCHERRY EUGENIA (*Eugenia paniculata australis, E. myrtifolia*). Good evergreen for sandy soil in the South and California. Bushy, with whitish flowers blooming throughout year, purplish fruit, reddish foliage.

AUSTRALIAN PINE; HORSEBALL TREE (*Casuarina equisetifolia*). Vigorous evergreen for the South and California with drooping branches, globular cones; tolerates close clipping.

BAY; LAUREL WILLOW (*Salix pentandra*). Deciduous, hardy to extreme North, with attractive, glossy, 5-inch-long, finely toothed leaves; catkins.

BLACKHAW (*Viburnum prunifolium*). Deciduous, hardy to extreme North. Makes thick, dense hedge, good clipped or unclipped; white flowers. To 15 feet.

BLACKTHORN; SLOE (*Prunus spinosa*). Deciduous in North. A thorny bush or tree to 12 feet with many small leaves, small white flowers followed by blue-black small fruit. Makes dense thorny hedge.

BUCKTHORN (*Rhamnus cathartica*). Deciduous; as hardy as they come. Makes thick, dense spiny hedge with occasional trimming. The stand-by for hedges in extreme North.

CANADA HEMLOCK (*Tsuga canadensis*). Evergreen, hardy to extreme North. Hardiest of the hemlocks, makes very graceful handsome evergreen hedge. Prefers shade; clips well.

CAROLINA CHERRY LAUREL (*Prunus caroliniana*). Evergreen for the South and California with glossy foliage, small white flowers. Also known as **Wild Orange** and **Mock Orange** in some sections in the country.

COCKSPUR THORN (*Crataegus Crus-galli*). Deciduous, hardy to extreme North. Thorny glossy foliage of excellent substance.

DOUGLAS FIR (*Pseudotsuga taxifolia*). Dark bluish evergreen, hardy to extreme North, one of the noblest timber trees. Makes stout dense hedge, stands pruning well. Cones to 4½ inches long.

ENGLISH HAWTHORN (*Crataegus Oxyacantha*). Hardy, deciduous, with thorny, inch-long spines. Makes impenetrable tall screen. To 15 feet.

EUROPEAN BEECH (*Fagus sylvatica*). Deciduous, hardy, unequaled for tall dense hedge; slow-growing with shining dark-green leaves turning red-brown in fall. Excellent winter windbreak too. If pruned, retains most of its leaves in winter.

EUROPEAN EUONYMUS (*Euonymus europaeus*). Deciduous, hardy to extreme North. Excellent for shade, makes dense hedge with dark-green foliage.

GRAY BIRCH (*Betula populifolia*). Deciduous, hardy to extreme North. Makes superb hedge, chalky bark, wrapped in foliage from top to ground. Stands winds; relatively resistant to birch borer.

HUNGARIAN LILAC (*Syringa Josikaea*). Deciduous, hardy to extreme North. An outstanding lilac for hedges, with glossy foliage, lilac panicles to 7 inches long. Relatively free from insects and disease.

ITALIAN CYPRESS (*Cupressus sempervirens*). Dark green evergreen for the South and California. Of tall columnar habit with cones to 1½ inches across. Clips well.

JAPANESE HOLLY (*Ilex crenata*). Evergreen, hardy shrub, to 20 feet, with flowers in May, June, followed by black berries. Easy to grow and to transplant.

JAPANESE LILAC (*Syringa japonica*). Hardy, deciduous with cream-white flowers in panicles to 12 inches long.

LATE HONEYSUCKLE (*Lonicera Maackii podocarpa*). Deciduous, hardy, with persistent dark-green foliage. Of spreading habit, with white flowers changing to yellow.

LAWSON CYPRESS (*Chamaecyparis Lawsoniana vars.*). Evergreen for the South and California, though unsatisfactory in dry climate. Popular, prized for its very ornamental form; has drooping branches of gray-green foliage; cones ⅓ inch across. Clips well, hardy in central states. Some forms even stand sheltered position in southern New England.

LILAC (*Syringa villosa*). Deciduous, hardy, a good hedge lilac with typical lilac or pinkish white flowers in terminal panicles 1 foot long.

LILAC (*Syringa vulgaris*). Deciduous, hardy to extreme North, dense. A very popular, pretty, inexpensive, informal hedge with fragrant panicles of lilac, pinkish, purplish or white flowers.

NORWAY SPRUCE (*Picea Abies*). Hardy evergreen with drooping, dark-green, glossy leaves. One of the most commonly planted in North America. Fast growing, develops naturally into hedge—uniform, broad at base and narrowing at top.

PYRAMID EUROPEAN HORNBEAM (*Carpinus Betulus fastigiata*). Deciduous, hardy. Slow-growing, dense and twiggy with fruiting catkins to 6 inches long. Clips well. Of pyramidal habit.

RED CEDAR (*Juniperus virginiana*). Hardy evergreen with scalelike and overlapping or needlelike and spreading leaves. Clips well, shears well. Color varies. Be sure to get a good match.

ROSE OF SHARON (*Hibiscus syriacus*). Deciduous, hardy. A popular informal flowering hedge with large showy flowers, rose or purple to white, bluish.

SAWARA CYPRESS (*Chamaecyparis pisifera vars.*). Evergreen, hardy to the extreme North. Mainly golden yellow; many tall growing; widely variable.

SERBIAN SPRUCE (*Picea Omorika*). Evergreen, hardy, with beautiful dense foliage. 2-inch-long flattened leaves with 2 white bands above, glossy dark green below; cones to 2½ inches long.

SHINGLE OAK (*Quercus imbricaria*). Hardy, deciduous. One of the most successful hedges. Long, oblong dark-green leaves turn yellowish brown, to brown, and remain all winter to act as windbreak.

SIBERIAN PEA TREE (*Caragana arborescens*). Deciduous, hardy to extreme North, with yellow-green leaves; yellow flowers in May, June. Resistant to heat and drought. Leafs early.

SIDNEY GOLDEN WATTLE (*Acacia longifolia*). Evergreen for the South and California, with pretty, loose flower spikes. Tolerant to poor conditions.

SPIREA, VANHOUTTE (*Spiraea Vanhouttei*). Deciduous, hardy. Makes a gracefull tall hedge up to 6 to 8 feet if left unpruned. Leaves bluish green. Masses of pure white flowers on crowded twiggy shoots, arresting display in spring.

TATARIAN HONEYSUCKLE (*Lonicera tatarica*). Deciduous, hardy to extreme North. A rapid inexpensive grower. If not sheared, bears pink or white flowers in May, June, followed by red fruit.

WASHINGTON THORN (*Crataegus Phaenopyrum*). Deciduous, hardy, of nice straight upright growth; fine, shiny foliage. Spines 3 inches long.

WHITE PINE (*Pinus Strobus*). Evergreen, hardy to extreme North, one of the finest where a tall hedge is desired. 5-inch-long blue-green leaves in cluster of 5 with long cone to 4 inches. Shearing can keep it 5 to 8 feet.

WINGED EUONYMUS (*Euonymus alatus*). Deciduous hardy shrub to 8 feet with finely toothed leaves, purplish fruit. Superb in fall when leaves turn rosy scarlet; of interest in winter because of corky-ridged branches. Easy to transplant.

YAUPON; CASSENA (*Ilex vomitoria*). Evergreen for the South and California with dense foliage, scarlet berries. Clips well.

Index to Plants

B

C

E

F

G

M

Q

R

T

U

V

W